Home Décor Sewing Techniques BIBLE

Home
Décor
Sewing
Techniques
BIBLE

Julia Bunting

Cincinnati, Ohio
www.mycraftivity.com

A QUARTO BOOK

First published in North America
in 2009 by Krause Publications,
an imprint of F+W Media, Inc.
4700 East Galbraith Road
Cincinnati, Ohio 45236

Copyright © 2009 Quarto Inc.

Library of Congress Catalog
information applied for.
ISBN-10: 0-89689-802-4
ISBN-13: 978-0-89689-802-8

QUAR.SFB

Conceived, designed, and produced by
Quarto Publishing plc
The Old Brewery
6 Blundell Street
London N7 9BH

Senior editor Katie Hallam
Copy editor Diana Chambers
Art editor and designer Julie Francis
Managing art editor Anna Plucinska
Art director Caroline Guest
Design assistant Saffron Stocker
Picture researcher Sarah Bell

Illustrator Kuo Kang Chen
Photographer Simon Pask

Art director Moira Clinch
Publisher Paul Carslake

Color separation by Modern Age
Printed in China by Midas Printing
                    International Ltd.

10 9 8 7 6 5 4 3 2 1

Contents

Introduction

I was drawn to the world of home décor by the small delicate floral prints of the 1980s. Fabric designs have come a long way since then, but their beauty and versatility still hold my interest.

In the past, curtains often had to be heavy, fully lined, and interlined to provide warmth and protection from drafty windows. They often dominated the room. With more effective windows and insulation a less formal, contemporary style has emerged, allowing curtains to become a true design feature. Less fabric is required for many of the recent ideas for window treatments, so a touch of glamor can be brought affordably into your home, along with the opportunity to change styles and colors more often.

In this book you will find a wealth of general information about home décor, detailed step-by-step instructions for many individual projects, and the sewing techniques required to make them. You'll also find practical advice to help you to select the appropriate choice for your window, whether it's French doors or a small bathroom recess.

It gives me the greatest pleasure to pass on tips that I've learned over the years and I hope you will feel a real sense of achievement when you have completed your individual project. Remember that preparation is key: measure and cut accurately, and choose your fabric with care. And don't forget to enjoy the fruits of your labor.

Julia Bunting

About this book

The first chapters of this book provide information to help you get started and make the projects in the chapters that follow. Toward the back of the book, you'll find inspirational sections providing guidance on style and fabric.

Window treatments
pages 60–115

Skill level indicates whether the project is best suited to beginners (1) or advanced sewers (3)

Introduction explains the key aspects of the project

Each project is broken down into easy-to-follow steps

Clear illustrations clarify the main stages

References are given to other relevant techniques in the book

Images focus on specific detail

All the tools and materials you need to make the project are listed

The finished item is displayed at the end of each project

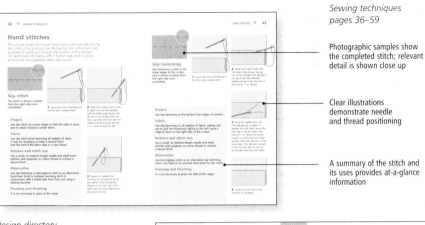

Sewing techniques
pages 36–59

Photographic samples show
the completed stitch; relevant
detail is shown close up

Clear illustrations
demonstrate needle
and thread positioning

A summary of the stitch and
its uses provides at-a-glance
information

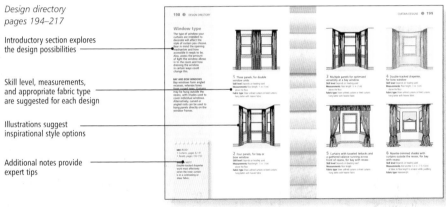

Design directory
pages 194–217

Introductory section explores
the design possibilities

Skill level, measurements,
and appropriate fabric type
are suggested for each design

Illustrations suggest
inspirational style options

Additional notes provide
expert tips

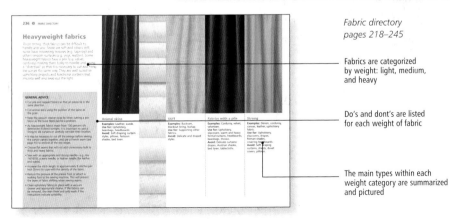

Fabric directory
pages 218–245

Fabrics are categorized
by weight: light, medium,
and heavy

Do's and dont's are listed
for each weight of fabric

The main types within each
weight category are summarized
and pictured

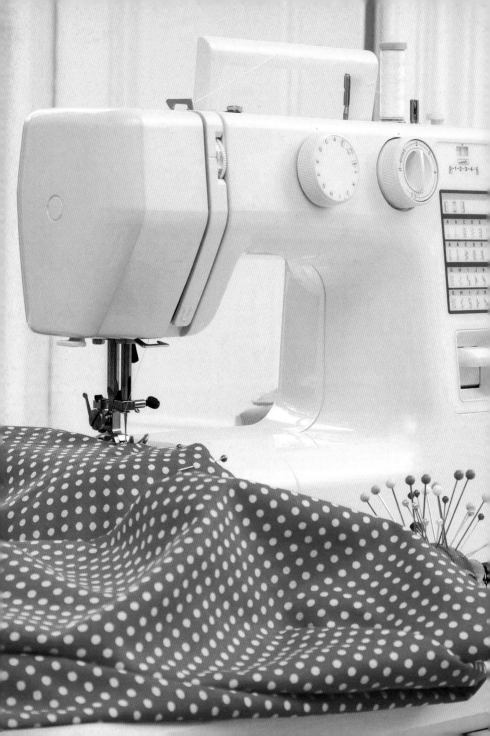

Tools and materials

It is a good idea to assemble the correct tools and materials before you start working. Prepare a workspace with a table or workbench, good natural light, and access to electric sockets. Easy access to an iron and ironing board will also save you time. Try to purchase the best tools you can afford as they will outlast cheaper ones and will help you to achieve a professional finish. The following pages look at the key pieces of equipment in a home decorator's kit.

Tools

Whether it's having the right pair of scissors for each cutting task or the appropriate suspension system for your window treatment, using the correct equipment will save time and give a better finish.

Sewing machines

Today's modern sewing machines are very different from those hand-powered, straight-stitch machines our mothers used. Computer technology now allows for numerous stitches to be pre-programmed, making functional, decorative, and embroidery stitching very simple. Although machines and models vary, they all work in the same basic way.

1 Bobbin winder This winds the thread speedily and evenly on to the bobbin.

2 Thread spindle This may be horizontal or vertical and holds the reel of thread.

3 Thread guides These hold the threads in the correct route before reaching the needle.

4 Needle This is held in place with a screw for easy changing.

5 Bobbin holder The bobbin is placed in its holder under the throat plate. It releases the thread under tension, allowing the thread to link with the needle thread to form a stitch.

6 Throat plate This surrounds the feed dogs and covers the bobbin and bobbin holder, forming a flat surface. The needle travels down through the throat plate to pick up the bobbin thread below.

7 Presser foot The presser foot is lowered to hold the fabric in position while stitches are formed.

8 Feed dogs The "teeth" grab the fabric and move it according to the length of stitch required.

9 Stitch selection Buttons, dials, or a touch-sensitive screen allow selection of the stitch required.

10 Fly wheel The fly wheel or balance wheel can be turned by hand to raise or lower the needle.

11 Pedal The foot pedal operates the machine at an appropriate speed. Sometimes an on/off button and a sliding switch on the machine will do this too.

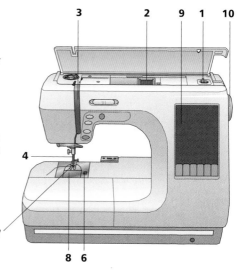

Sergers/overlockers

These have become popular in recent years as they allow home sewers to benefit from a manufactured seam finish. They also produce wonderful creative seams and edges, and sew modern stretch fabrics with ease.

1 Thread spindles There are four of these on most sergers. The two on the left feed the needles and the two on the right feed the loopers.

2 Thread guides These hold the threads in the correct routes before reaching the needles and loopers.

3 Tension dials These allow the threads to be adjusted and so form different types of stitch, for example, a balanced stitch, flatlocking, and rolled hemming.

4 Needles There are normally two needles on a serger. They may both be used for four-thread serging. Wide three-thread serging is made with the left needle in position. Narrow serging uses the right needle only.

5 Loopers The loopers feed the threads below the needles and allow stitches to be formed when they link with the needle threads.

6 Knives The knives cut off the excess fabric before the threads form stitches over the cut edge.

7 Fly wheel The fly wheel or balance wheel can be turned by hand to raise or lower the needles.

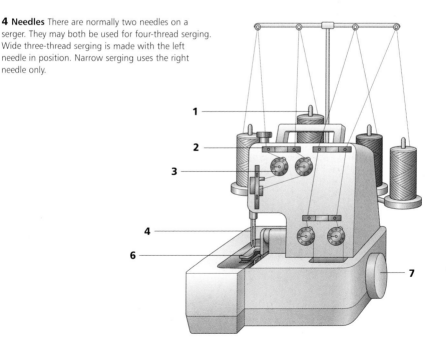

Machine feet and attachments

Most sewing machines will be supplied with a small selection of feet to aid particular sewing tasks. These will normally include a standard foot, a zipper foot, and a buttonhole foot, but there are many others available. They may vary in appearance from one make to another but are designed specifically to make each task easier.

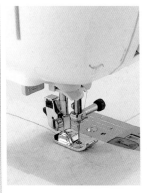

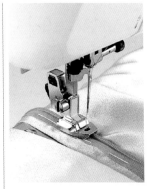

Straight stitch foot

Used for: Straight stitching (especially on fine fabric)

Sewer's notes: Replace the normal (wide hole) throat plate with a (small hole) straight stitch throat plate. This, and the straight stitch foot, holds the fabric closer to the needle and prevents it from being pushed down and jamming the mechanism.

Concealed zipper foot

Used for: Inserting concealed/invisible zippers

Sewer's notes: Use the standard zipper foot on the outer edge of the zipper tape to secure it first, then feed the teeth into the concealed foot. This gets right under the teeth and the zipper will be invisible in the seam.

Walking foot

Used for: Long seams, hems on stretch fabric, multiple fabric layers, patchwork

Sewer's notes: This is one of the most useful feet available. The foot walks over the cloth and prevents seams from shifting along its length or stretching. Use when accuracy is essential for matching large patterns or patchwork pieces, and for stitching blackout lining as it prevents slippage.

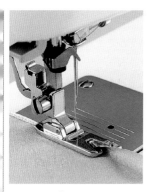

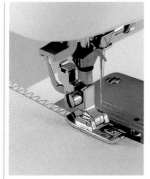

Narrow hem or picot foot

Used for: Narrow rolled hemming
Sewer's notes: Machine a row of straight stitches close to the edge and trim up to it. Feed this edge into the rolled hem foot, which turns it and stitches the hem. Use a straight stitch or zigzag. Available in various widths.

Overcasting foot

Used for: Neatening edges and sewing serge-like seams
Sewer's notes: The "finger" on the foot allows stitches to be formed over it without pulling on the fabric edge. Cut away the excess with shears and feed the cut edge under the finger. Use with a pre-programmed overcast stitch or zigzag.

Gathering foot

Used for: For ruffles and frills
Sewer's notes: Set the machine to a long straight stitch and place the fabric to be gathered uppermost. Feed the other layer in through the guide in the foot with right side down. The lower layer will be gathered and stitched to the upper layer.

Pin tuck foot

Used for: Creating twin-needle tucks to decorate fabric
Sewer's notes: A row of twin-needle tucks can be fed under the grooves of the foot, allowing further tucks to be made close and parallel to the first.

Clear foot

Used for: Appliqué, embroidery, and where it is helpful to view the stitching
Sewer's notes: The clear foot often has a wide groove on the underside to help it glide over decorative stitching.

10 tips and hints

Following a few simple steps will help you get the most from your sewing machine/serger.

1 Setting up

Place the machine in a well-lit area on a large surface to give plenty of room to work. Make sure the seating is of a suitable type and height for you to sew comfortably.

2 Machine maintenance

Keep the sewing machine or serger lint- and dust-free. A build-up of lint can jam the mechanism or get caught beneath the stitches.

3 Needles

Replace needles frequently and use the type designed for the task. This will eliminate skipped stitches and damage to fabric threads.

7 Bobbins

Wind bobbins carefully and steadily. Bobbins wound too fast can cause puckered seams and if wound unevenly, stitch tension may be poor or threads may break.

8 Secure thread ends

Fasten off thread ends by a) threading them on to a needle and securing them, b) using a product to fuse or glue them, c) tie them in a knot, or d) reverse stitch at the beginning and end of stitching.

9 Leave a tail of threads to start

If the sewing machine does not automatically cut the threads, always leave a tail behind the needle. Otherwise, as the needle is raised to start sewing again the thread may come out of the eye.

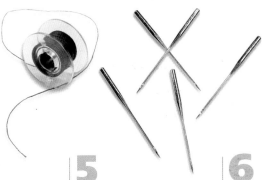

4

Thread

Always use good quality thread. It should be evenly spun with long fibers to travel easily through the guides and produce a minimum of lint.

5

Feet and attachments

Make use of specialist presser feet. They will make the task easier and quicker as well as produce a better finished result.

6

Trial stitching

Always make a trial first to eliminate problems and find the best stitch length and width before handling a project. Different fabrics sew in different ways and adjustments may be necessary.

10

Speed

Sew at a steady speed to produce even stitching. This is especially important for decorative work as stitches will not be formed accurately if the speed is too fast or erratic.

Measuring tools

It is essential to measure projects accurately to produce a professional finish and then to measure the fabric precisely before cutting out. You will need a selection of tools to complete most home décor projects.

1 Retractable steel measure

This is probably the most important item you will need in your tool kit. It is used to provide accurate measurements of windows and also to measure the fabric to make curtains and shades. It will give a fixed measurement, but is flexible when measuring beds and curved items.

2 Measurement gauge

This handy gadget allows small measurements to be checked easily. It is marked on both sides and is easy to manipulate when folding up hems, marking buttonholes, and positioning top stitching.

3 Tape measure

Choose a good quality tape measure that will neither ravel nor stretch. It should be at least 60 in. (150cm) long with clear measurements marked from the start of the tape. It is possible to purchase a tape measure up to 120 in. (300cm) long.

4 Sewing gauge

This is a ruler with a sliding marker, used to fix measurements for pleats, hems, and tucks.

5 Yard (meter) stick

Made of wood or metal, a stick is ideal for measuring lengths of fabric from a roll. The stable nature of a yard (meter) stick is good for marking straight lengths for cushions etc.

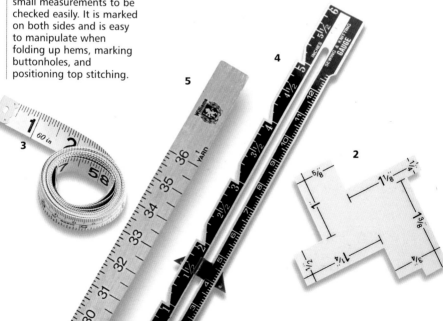

Cutting tools

A variety of shapes and sizes of scissors perform different tasks, all helping to make the sewing project easier. Choose good quality tools and look after them, sharpening or replacing them when necessary.

1 Scissors/shears

Sharp, long-bladed scissors are ideal for cutting fabric quickly and with a smooth edge. Use long sweeping cuts to give a straight edge. Sidebent scissors have a lower blade that lies flat on the table and an upper blade that moves to cut the fabric. Although useful, they are not essential. Select scissors that are made with stainless steel blades that will not rust. Only use these scissors on fabric as they will be blunted if you use them to cut paper. Left-handed and soft-handled shears are also available.

2 Paper scissors

It is essential to have a pair of scissors that you use only for cutting paper, as using fabric shears for cutting paper patterns will blunt them and they will no longer cut your fabric neatly. Scissors for cutting paper do not need to have sharp points.

3 Needlework/ embroidery scissors

Scissors with short blades and sharp points are very useful. The sharp points can be used for cutting individual stitches or for getting into difficult corners for trimming.

4 Quick unpick

A quick unpick or seam ripper is useful when removing a line of stitching. Either separate the seam and unpick the stitches or cut every third stitch on one side, then turn the seam over and pull out the thread from the other side. Use the tool to cut buttonholes open by placing a pin across one end and cutting from the other end up to the pin.

5 Thread snips

These are for cutting threads only, so keep them by your sewing machine.

Ironing and pressing tools

An iron is essential for pressing seams open, creasing fabric edges and hems and holding them in place, and producing a sharp edge on cushions and a smooth finish on curtains and blinds.

Dry iron

A dry iron can be used in conjunction with a damp cloth or water-bottle spray when required. Care must be taken, though, as some fabrics are permanently damaged by water marks.

Steam iron

A steam iron contains a small amount of water and pushes steam through the cloth, which makes ironing more efficient. It is easy to use and gives a good finish.

Tank iron

A tank iron has a large reservoir of water connected by a pipe to the iron. This type of iron produces a greater pressure of steam than a normal steam iron.

Pressing cloths

Pieces of cotton muslin are perfect for protecting your fabric from an iron's heat. You can also purchase chemically treated pressing cloths that give a crisp professional finish.

Ironing board

A large ironing board is useful as it can be used as an extra work surface when working on small items such as tiebacks, valances, or pelmets. It is also a good idea to have a board that has an adjustable height as pressing finished curtains can be a long job and having the board at the correct height makes the job much easier.

Pins and needles

Using the correct pins and needles can save hours of frustration. The wrong machine needle can lead to skipped stitches, pulled threads, or can even break under the strain.

1

4

5

1 Glass-headed/ pearl-headed pins

These are useful for most sewing projects with the advantage that if they are dropped on the floor they can easily be seen and picked up. They are less likely to fall out of loosely woven fabrics and are easier to push through layers of thick fabric without hurting your fingers. Take care if the pinhead is plastic as it will melt if it comes into contact with the iron.

3

2 Quilter's pins

These long pins are used for quilting and can secure several thick layers together.

3 Craft pins

These long strong pins are used with buckram and pelmet-weight interfacing. They have large heads that make it easy to secure thick layers together.

4 Flower-head pins

These long pins with large flat heads are ideal for loosely woven fabrics like lace, net, and other sheer fabrics.

5 Safety pins

Use safety pins when ordinary pins are likely to fall out. Also used for feeding elastic through slots.

2

Hand needles

There are many different hand needles to suit various tasks. Here is a selection that will be useful in your home décor projects.

Sharps
These are fine, medium-length needles with small eyes for general stitching. The longer, thicker ones are used for attaching buckram to curtain fabric.

Betweens
Betweens are small, thin needles with small eyes for fine sewing and delicate stitching.

Bodkins
Bodkins are large, blunt needles designed to thread elastic or cord through casings.

Machine needles

A variety of machine needles are used to suit different fabrics.

1 Standard/universal
These are used for general stitching. The point is sharp enough to pierce woven fabric and round enough to push between the yarns of knitted cloth. They are available in different sizes; the lower number ratings are for finer fabrics.

Microtex
Use microtex needles for silk and microfiber fabrics. The sharp point penetrates woven fabrics.

Ball point
Ball-point needles are designed for knitted fabrics. The needle pushes between the yarns of the cloth rather than splitting them.

2 Quilting
A quilting needle has a long sharp point to stitch through several layers together.

Top stitch needles
Top stitch needles have larger eyes and grooves than standard needles. The eye is big enough to take two strands of ordinary thread or top stitching, buttonhole, or machine embroidery floss.

Jeans
Jeans needles are strong with a sharp point to penetrate heavy, thick fabrics like denim, canvas, or upholstery cloth.

1

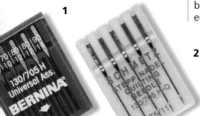

2

1 Thimble

The humble thimble is one of the most important items in your sewing kit. It is made from metal or sometimes plastic. It usually fits onto the middle finger and is used when hand sewing. It helps to push the needle through fabrics, can be used when pinning thick fabrics together, and can also be used to push pin hooks into pinch pleat-headed curtains.

2 Table clamps or weights

Table clamps are used to secure fabric to the edges of the workbench when cutting out slippery fabrics or when the fabric is heavy and will not stay in place on a flat surface. Alternatively, weights can be used.

Markers

Marking tools are important when producing a home décor item. They are used to show the positions of tucks and pleats and also to indicate the face side of the fabric when cutting several lengths of curtain fabric. Always mark the top of each piece so that the pile or nap runs in the same direction.

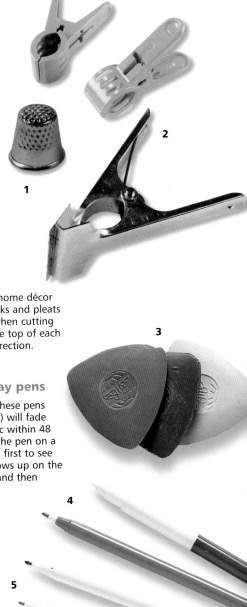

3 Chalk

Chalk is traditionally used for marking cloth and can be brushed off afterward. Chalk comes in triangular pieces, rollers, and pencils in various colors. Keep the edges or points sharp and choose a color that will show up well on the fabric.

4 Washaway pens

The ink from these pens (normally blue) can be wiped off later with a damp cloth. It is advisable to try it out on a scrap of fabric first to check that water doesn't damage the cloth.

5 Fade-away pens

The ink from these pens (normally pink) will fade from the fabric within 48 hours. Check the pen on a scrap of fabric first to see whether it shows up on the chosen cloth and then disappears.

Suspension systems

Suspension systems are the fixings used to attach the curtains or shades to the window. There are two main categories—functional and decorative. Functional fixings are usually essential and decorative ones are attractive and form a large part of the overall appearance.

Rods

Tracks

Tracks tend to be functional and are concealed, whenever possible, with valances or pelmets. Concealed rods vary in function; many are designed to solve specific problems. Rods that swivel allow you to curtain inward-opening casements or French doors without interference or obstruction; angled or curved rods fit inside the recess of a bay. With this type of hardware, practicality may be the sole criterion for selection.

Tracks tend to be made of plastic for light- to mediumweight curtains, and steel or aluminum for medium- to heavyweight curtains, and can be corded for ease of use.

In the case of decorative hardware, style and material broaden the choice immensely. A style can be chosen that complements both the window treatment itself and the architectural detailing of the room.

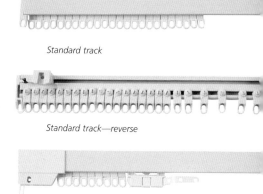

Standard track

Standard track—reverse

Corded track

Rollers and gliders move along the track allowing smooth operation. The better quality ones can reduce noise too.

Some modern suspension systems give the look of a pole but are in fact tracks.

A strong aluminum track is advisable for hanging heavy full-length curtains.

Poles

Wooden and metal poles are available in a wide variety of finishes and styles, from traditional to contemporary. Wooden poles may be stained, painted, gilded, or varnished. Metal rods offer a similar range of choice from country-style rustic to modern polished chrome. Finials, which form the end piece of the poles, come in a huge variety of shapes and sizes, and may be made from a contrasting material such as glass or stone.

Finials can be a decorative feature in their own right, but it is important that they reflect the style of the room.

Brackets should match the pole and are drilled into the wall to secure.

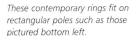

These contemporary rings fit on rectangular poles such as those pictured bottom left.

Rings are made to match the style and material of the pole. Some are available with a nylon lining (right) so they don't make a noise when used.

An easy fix for lightweight curtains or even a piece of fabric you want to use as a curtain is pincer clips, which simply grasp the top of the fabric, so no heading tape is required.

Colored rings can blend into the interior scheme or can be used to accentuate other features, such as the holdbacks and rug featured here.

Battens, headrails, and sidewinders

For Roman shades, there are three main lifting mechanisms.

1 The simplest and cheapest method is a wooden batten, screw eyes, and cords.
2 The corded aluminum headrail has movable cord guides and a cord-locking device at one end.
3 The sidewinder system has movable tape reels, a drive shaft, and a rotary chain at one end. This is the most expensive fixing but will hold the heaviest blinds and provides a neat finish.

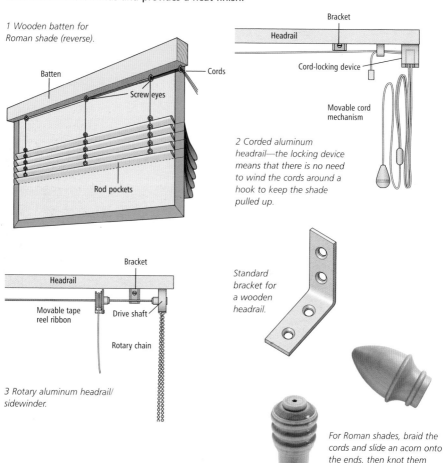

1 Wooden batten for Roman shade (reverse).

Batten

Screw eyes

Cords

Rod pockets

Bracket

Headrail

Cord-locking device

Movable cord mechanism

2 Corded aluminum headrail—the locking device means that there is no need to wind the cords around a hook to keep the shade pulled up.

Bracket

Headrail

Movable tape reel ribbon

Drive shaft

Rotary chain

3 Rotary aluminum headrail/ sidewinder.

Standard bracket for a wooden headrail.

For Roman shades, braid the cords and slide an acorn onto the ends, then knot them together to keep the cords tidily tucked away, ensuring ease of use.

Pelmet boards and valances

Pelmet boards are constructed from wood and will be fixed above the window and track with angle brackets. The pelmet is attached with a touch-and-close fastener.

Valances can also be attached in this way, or onto a valance track with hooks that can be combined with the curtain track.

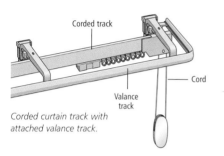

Corded track

Cord

Valance track

Corded curtain track with attached valance track.

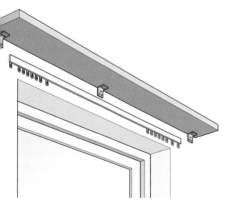

Wooden pelmet board.

It is essential that a good stiffener is used to back the pelmet fabric, as it will enable the pelmet to keep its shape and smooth finish.

Fabric

There is an endless number of designs, textures, qualities, and colors of fabric available from which to choose for home décor projects. The correct choice of fabric is important to achieve the most satisfying outcome for all the hard work that will be put into any project.

Warm colors include reds, ochre yellows, terra-cottas, and olive greens. They create a warm atmosphere and are ideal for rooms in which there is a lot of activity, such as kitchens and living rooms.

Cool colors include blues, blue-greens, and lilacs. They create a restful, quiet atmosphere and are a great choice for bathrooms and bedrooms.

Neutrals include white, cream, oatmeal, taupe, and black and can be used together in a neutral scheme (above) or in warm or cool schemes. These colors break up or neutralize stronger colors.

Color

For any home décor project, you'll need a color range to work with, and collecting samples of fabric and looking at them in the relevant room will give the best possible outcome. Ultimately the color scheme you choose is down to you, but it's a good idea to be familiar with the categories of color and the moods they can create.

NOTE
For more information on fabric, see the Fabric directory on pages 218–245.

Weight

Heavier fabrics, such as velvet and textured cottons, are better suited to full-length, structured, formal curtains with pinch-pleated or goblet-pleated headings that mold the fabric into deep folds. Lightweight fabrics, such as chintz and voiles, are more suited to simple gathered headings, making casual, breezy curtains. When choosing your fabric, consider how it will hang—whether it has a soft drape that would hang well as a curtain, or if it is crisp and unyielding, and therefore best suited to shades.

Lining and interlining will alter a fabric's weight and may alter its drape. Lining adds body to a flimsy fabric, whereas interlining—a layer of soft batting that lies between the face fabric and the lining—adds weight, thickness, and body, to create luxuriously heavy curtains.

BUYER'S GUIDE

For most of us, home décor can represent a significant expenditure, so wrong decisions can prove costly. Once you've chosen your fabric, there are some guidelines you can follow when purchasing it that should help to prevent expensive mistakes.

- **Before you buy** It's worth obtaining or purchasing a large sample of your chosen fabric to take home and see how it looks in the light of your room. Small swatches can be misleading.

- **Shed some light** In-store, roll out a length to assess the impact of color and pattern. View the fabric in natural light to gain an idea of true color values. Hold translucent or lace fabrics up to the light to assess sheerness and pattern, if any.

- **Take a good look** Examine the fabric for flaws or unacceptable marks.

- **Try it out** Gather or pleat the fabric in your hands to assess the effect of different types of heading on the pattern and weave.

- **Check the label** A fabric's fiber content, weave structure, and finish are the main factors determining how the fabric will perform. This information can generally be found on the fabric label.

- **Don't fall short** Make sure you buy enough fabric to finish the job. Colors may vary from batch to batch, which could make subsequent matching difficult.

Texture

Texture affects the way that light plays on a fabric—the sheen of chintz, the nap of velvet, and the shimmer of some synthetic fibers are brought to life by the varying intensity of both natural and artificial light.

Patterns

Patterns on textiles can be woven, printed, or embroidered.

Woven designs include traditional and formal brocades and damask, as well as more "utilitarian" stripes, plaids, and checks.

Printed designs are usually applied to flat, nontextured fabrics, which can be silk, cotton, and linen.

Embroidered fabrics range from traditional, handmade crewelwork through to intricately embroidered silks and machine-embroidered cottons and linens. They are almost always floral in design.

When considering patterned fabric for curtains, remember that the flat sample in the pattern book will look different when it is hung in the folds and pleats of a curtain. Stripes will look less rigid, bold patterns will be softened, and some small patterns may be lost.

Sundry materials

1 Threads

Using the correct thread is very important. Polyester is an excellent choice as it is fine, strong, and comes in a fantastic range of colors. Basting threads are soft cotton and break easily for temporary stitching and will not damage the fabric when they are removed. Silk thread can be used on silk fabric but is expensive. Clear thread can be used on some sheer fabrics when the stitching lines will become invisible.

2 Linings

Most curtains and blinds benefit from the addition of lining. It improves the life of the fabric and the drape of the curtain. It protects from sunlight damage, absorbs condensation, and adds to the insulation properties of the drapes.

Cotton sateen is the most popular lining choice. It is a tightly woven cotton with a slight sheen. It comes commonly in white, cream, and ecru, but is also available in a variety of colors. It is always sensible to buy a good quality lining as it will retain its body after cleaning and give a much better appearance.

3 Blackout lining

Blackout lining is available in cream and white and has a rubberized backing. It is useful in bedrooms and nurseries. It can also be used for lining Roman shades as it will block out the light on a single flat layer of the face fabric.

Blackout lining makes curtains heavy, so will require a secure fixing when several widths of fabric are used. It also requires a higher skill level during construction. Using a walking foot on the sewing machine can help when joining widths of blackout lining together.

1

2

3

4 Interlining

Inserting a layer of interlining between the fabric and lining produces a sumptuous effect and makes curtains hang beautifully. It can also be used to add texture to Roman shades. Interlining is usually made from natural cotton, but man-made synthetic interlining is also available and is generally cheaper. It comes in various weights depending on how thick or heavy the finished curtains are intended to be.

Domette is brushed cotton, medium in weight, and can be used in curtains and shades. The finished curtains will be heavy, so a substantial fixing will be required.

4

5 Pillow forms

There are many types of pillow forms. Feather, synthetic fiberfill, kapok, and solid foam (usually for box cushions) are all available and in many sizes. Feather forms give the best appearance and will not lose their shape, but they are not always practical as the feathers can cause allergic reactions. However, an extra cover can be made to enclose the feather form to stop the feathers from coming through.

5

Heading tapes

A wide range of heading tapes is available in various materials suitable for different fabrics. They all serve one purpose, which is to gather up the top of the curtain or valance to the required measurement. This is done by means of cords threaded through the length of the tape. The tape has rows of pockets in which hooks are evenly placed to hang onto the track or pole.

Different designs can be created with different tapes. Simple standard gathering, smocking, pinch pleating, pencil pleating, and even box pleating can be achieved using sew-on tapes.

Net pleat tape

This translucent tape is used with lightweight nets and sheer fabrics. It can be used on a track, pole or stretchwire. It is made from 100 percent polyester, is 2 in. (50mm) wide and requires a minimum of double fullness.

Standard tape

This narrow tape is used for unlined, lined, or lightweight curtains. It can be used on a track or pole. It is made from 70 percent cotton and 30 percent polyester, is 1 in. (25mm) wide, and requires 1½–2 times fullness.

Triple pinch pleat tape

This elegant heading tape produces pinch pleats without hand sewing buckram into the curtain. The tape gives three pleats spaced evenly apart. It is made from 75 percent polyester and 25 percent polypropylene, is 3½ in. (88mm) wide, and requires double fullness. It does not give as crisp a finish as hand-stitched pleats and requires a special hook.

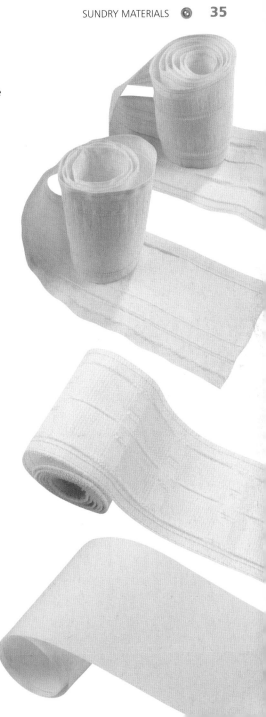

Goblet pleat tape

This tape automatically forms goblet-shaped pleats. It is commonly used on long curtains as it is a deep tape, and gives a stunning look. It is made from 68 percent polyester and 32 percent polypropylene, is 5 in. (138mm) wide, and requires double fullness for the fabric. Care must be taken when positioning the tape, so the goblets are not too close to the curtain edges.

Pencil pleat tape/ lightweight pencil pleat tape

This is a classic design that produces crisp, even, upright pleats that can be used with tracks and poles, and also for valances. It is made from 55 percent polyester and 45 percent polypropylene, is 3 in. (75mm) wide and requires 2–2½ times fullness. It is also available in a 6 in. (15cm) depth for long curtains.

Buckram

Buckram is a stiffened white cotton fabric and comes in widths of 4–6 in. (10–15cm). It is sewn into the top of curtains and valances to make decorative pleats. Fusible buckram is pressed rather than sewn to adhere to the fabric. However, it is not as easy to work with. Pin hooks are inserted into the heading for hanging.

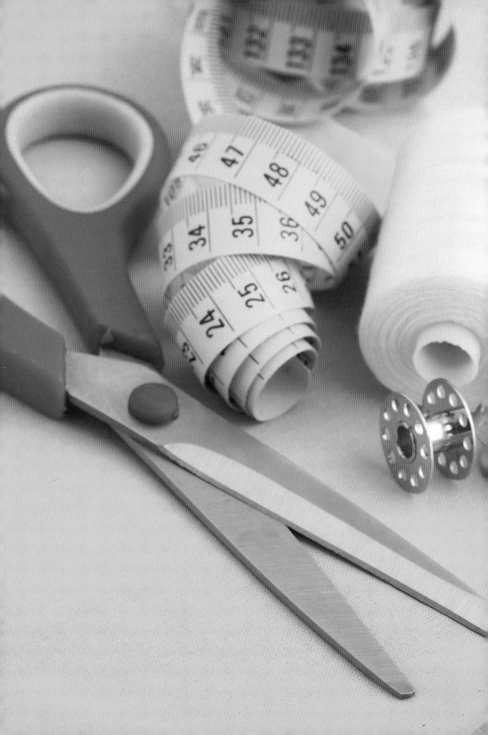

Sewing techniques

This chapter covers all the sewing techniques and stitches, both hand sewn and machine stitched, that you will need to make any of the home décor projects described in this book. It also details useful information about the fabric used for the various projects.

Fabric characteristics

Elements such as the grain of a fabric and its pattern are key when it comes to cutting, calculating amounts, and joining fabrics.

The grain

Before cutting out fabric for curtains or a shade, you need to check that the fabric is square, so that the curtains or shade will hang correctly. The straight or crosswise grain of the fabric should be at right angles to the selvage. Place the cut edge of the fabric on a table or cutting surface and support the rest of the fabric, so it does not distort the edge or slip off the table. Weight it down if necessary.

Straightening the edge on a plain woven fabric

METHOD 1

If you can see the individual threads and are able to cut along one of these threads from one selvage to the other, follow these instructions:

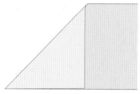

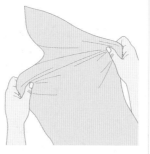

1. Having cut across the grain, replace the fabric against the edge of the table and if it is not at right angles to the edge, you may need to pull the fabric along the true bias. (Bias is any diagonal direction of the fabric, but true bias is the edge formed when you fold the fabric so that the lengthwise and crosswise grains match.)

2. Hold the corners that are diagonally opposite each other in your hands and pull firmly.

METHOD 2

On sheer or lightweight cotton fabrics, the fabric can be torn across the grain:

Snip into the selvage (about 1 in. [2.5cm]) and tear the fabric across the width, snipping off loose threads. Once the straight grain has been established, trim off the torn ragged edge to provide a neat cut edge.

Or

Snip the selvage and loosen a thread. It should be possible to ease out the thread and cut across the indentation formed.

METHOD 3

On a patterned fabric, the pattern must be followed across the width so it can be joined to the next length. Therefore, a slight tolerance away from the straight grain is allowed:

On the right side of the fabric use a line of pins or marker pen to indicate the cutting line across the fabric, following the pattern.

METHOD 4

Since most modern furnishing fabrics have a permanent, heat-set finish that locks the threads in position, it may not be possible to straighten the fabric in this way. In this instance:

Place the fabric onto the table and use a set square to achieve a right angle. Using a yard stick, continue the line and mark across to the other selvage.

THE SELVAGE

The selvage is the side edge of the fabric. It is tightly woven and will not ravel. It can, however, be extremely tight and should not be included in measurements for cushions, shades, and some other projects. Use it wherever possible as a straight edge and position cushion panels and shades parallel to the edge. It is usually kept on in curtain making but is snipped every 4–6 in. (10–15cm). Sometimes the selvages are necessary to complete pattern matching and therefore must be kept.

Pattern repeats

Some fabrics have a pattern repeat and must be cut so the pattern appears in the same position on each drop of fabric. The size of the pattern repeat can vary from 1 in. (2.5cm) to 40 in. (1m), but most are in multiples of 12½ in. (32cm).

Calculating the amount of fabric required

The pattern repeat must be taken into consideration. Once the top and bottom turnings have been added, round up the total to the next full repeat. For example, if the finished length of a pair of curtains is 80 in. (203cm), add 10 in. (25cm) for turnings, which gives a final length of 90 in. (229cm). If the pattern repeat is 25 in. (63cm), the amount required for each drop will be 100 in. (254cm). Multiply this by the number of widths required to reach the total requirement. With lining fabric, the pattern repeat does not have to be taken into consideration.

When working with a patterned fabric, it looks better if a pattern appears in full, starting (upward) from the bottom edge. At the top, the heading will mask a pattern that is not a full repeat.

On long curtains, the full pattern should start just below the heading as it will be most obvious at eye level.

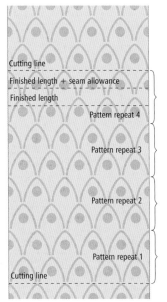

Cutting line

Finished length + seam allowance

Finished length

Pattern repeat 4

Pattern repeat 3

Pattern repeat 2

Pattern repeat 1

Cutting line

Joining seams

When you join two pieces of fabric together on a plain fabric, you should allow a 1 in. (2.5cm) seam allowance. This can include the selvage if it is not too tight. It may only be necessary to snip the selvage every 4–6 in. (10–15cm) so it will lay flat. On plain fabrics there may not be a color difference, but on printed fabrics the selvage may have a bold white edge, giving fabric composition and washing instructions. It may differ in width and, when you put the two pieces of fabric together, the two edges will not meet. This is not a problem, but if there is more than 1½ in. (3.8cm) on one side, the edge can be trimmed off.

Place the two pieces of fabric, right sides facing, on a flat surface and, starting from the bottom, pin together (see below).

When an odd number of widths is required, stitch a half-width to the outside edges. If there are only a few widths to join together (so they are not too heavy or bulky to handle), stitch them all together first and then cut up through the center of the middle width. This ensures that the half-width can always be placed correctly on the outside edge.

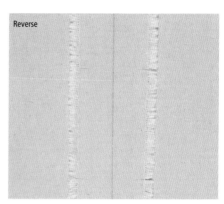

Reverse

Right side

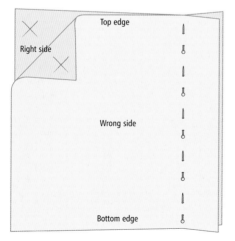

Top edge

Right side

Wrong side

Bottom edge

MARKING FABRIC AFTER CUTTING

When lengths of fabric are cut, it is important to make a mark on the top front side of each piece, which makes it easier to put the lengths together correctly. Certain fabrics, such as velvet and chenille, have a definite pile and will appear to be different colors if one is upside down. It is a good practice to mark every piece regardless of the pile so you never make a mistake. You can use a pin, a marker pen or chalk, or a colored thread.

Pattern matching

More work is involved when you need to join the widths together on patterned fabrics.

1. With right sides together, join the edges, starting at the bottom edge and working upward. Fold back the top edge and find a corresponding flower or design on the other piece. Crease the fold line with your fingers and replace.

2. Pin through the crease line. Open out the seam allowance to check that the pattern is matched correctly and adjust if necessary. Repeat on the next flower or design. Pin the fabrics together in between. It will become apparent that a straight line (for stitching) is forming.

Using a horizontal stripe, check, or geometric pattern

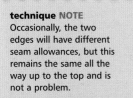

technique NOTE
Occasionally, the two edges will have different seam allowances, but this remains the same all the way up to the top and is not a problem.

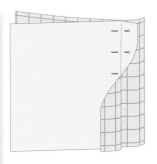

Pin the fabric together at right angles to the edge. This helps to keep the pattern match correct and can stop the fabric stretching when it is machined. Stitch over the horizontal pins carefully with a sewing machine. Check that the pattern matching is correct. You may need to unpick and restitch small sections. Snip the selvage every 4–6 in. (10–15cm) to take away the tightness and press the seam open.

Hand stitches

This section details functional hand stitches that are used during the construction process. Use the step-by-step instructions and diagrams to guide you through the creation of the stitches. The additional information offers further help, and machine alternatives are suggested where appropriate.

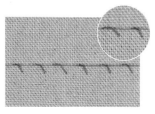

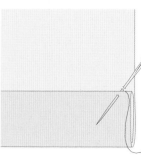

Slip stitch

This stitch is almost invisible from the right side once completed.

1. Secure the end of the thread in the fold with a double stitch.

2. Work from right to left (or left to right if you are left-handed) with the folded edge facing. Pick up one or two threads from the fabric just above the fold with the needle and slip through the hem ¼ in. (6mm) toward the left.

Project

Use slip stitch on curtain edges to hold the sides in place and to attach lining to curtain fabric.

Fabric

Use slip stitch when hemming all weights of fabric. It may be necessary to make a second stitch into the hem if the fabric slips or is very heavy.

Notions and stitch size

Use a small- to medium-length needle and small hand stitches with polyester or cotton thread to achieve a secure finish.

Alternative

Use slip hemming or herringbone stitch as an alternative hand-hem finish or a shade hemming stitch in conjunction with a shade hem foot if you are using a sewing machine.

Pressing and finishing

It is not necessary to press at this stage.

3. Repeat to complete the stitching. Do not pull the thread too tightly as this will pull the threads on the right side of the fabric and will cause indentations along the hem line.

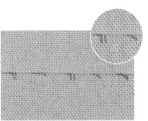

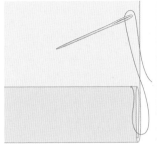

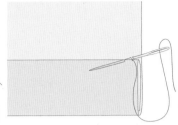

Slip hemming

Slip hemming is used on the lower edges of the curtain and is almost invisible from the right side once completed.

1. Secure the end of the thread in the fold with a double stitch.

2. Work from right to left with the folded edge facing. Pick up one or two threads from the fabric just above the fold with the needle and slip it into the fold of the hem for ¼ in. (6mm).

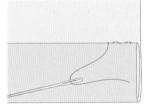

Project

Use slip hemming on the bottom hem edges of curtains.

Fabric

Use slip hemming on all weights of fabric, taking care not to pull the thread too tightly as this will cause a ridge to form on the right side of the curtain.

Notions and stitch size

Use a small- to medium-length needle and small stitches with polyester or cotton thread to achieve a secure finish.

Alternative

Use herringbone stitch as an alternative slip hemming stitch, but there is no machine alternative for this stitch.

Pressing and finishing

It is not necessary to press the hem at this stage.

3. Bring the needle out of the fold and pick up a couple of threads from the fabric above the fold. Slip it into the fold of the hem for ¼ in. (6mm). Bring the needle out of the fold and make another stitch into the hem in the same place. This will add strength to the hem but will not pull on the threads from the main fabric.

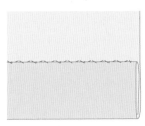

4. Continue to the end of the hem line to complete.

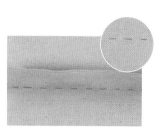

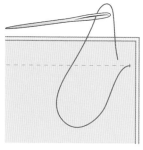

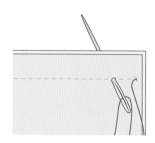

Basting/tacking

Basting or tacking is a row of long temporary stitches used to hold pieces of fabric together before machining.

1. Having secured the thread lightly on the wrong side, bring the needle through to the surface at the start of the first stitch.

2. Make a stitch ¼–½ in. (6–12mm) in length and take the needle down through the fabric.

Project

Basting is used whenever temporary stitching is required or when it is more difficult to secure layers of fabric together with pins. It is a good idea to use a different colored thread so that it easier to remove when the permanent stitching has been completed.

Fabric

Use on all weights of fabric.

Notions and stitch size

Use a medium-length needle. You can use cotton (rather than strong polyester) as it will break easily. Do not use a dark colored thread on a light background as it may stain the fabric.

Alternative

Use the longest stitch length when basting with the sewing machine.

Pressing and finishing

Do not iron basting stitches.

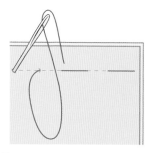

3. Continue to the end, making the stitches even on both the front and back of the work.

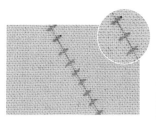

Ladder stitch

This stitch is used to join a seam together or, particularly in curtain making, to sew the corner together after making a miter on the hem edge.

1. On the corner of a curtain, pin the two mitered edges so that they sit together smoothly.

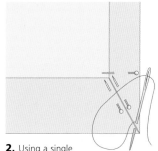

2. Using a single thread on the left edge (inside the miter), start with a couple of small stitches ¼ in. (6mm) from the corner. On the left side bring the needle up ⅛ in. (3mm) from the fold and go into the fold on the right, ⅛ in. (3mm) from the edge. Come up on the left through the same hole as before. Push the needle through the same hole on the right again and move downward ⅛ in. (3mm), coming up on the left. Make a double stitch across the corner.

Project

Ladder stitch is used on curtain hems to secure the mitered corner. It is also used on mitered corners after sewing buckram into the top of curtains and valances.

Fabric

Ladder stitch is used on all weights of fabric.

Notions and stitch size

A medium to long fine needle gives the best appearance. The stitches are small and firm to secure the closure over the lead weight. A fine polyester or cotton thread is suitable.

Alternative

There is no machine stitch alternative to ladder stitch, which must be stitched by hand from the reverse side of the curtain.

Pressing and finishing

Press gently on the reverse side of the fabric.

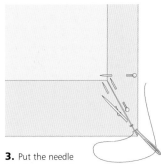

3. Put the needle into the same hole on the right-hand side and move up underneath the join and come out on the left side ¼ in. (6mm) up from the first stitch.

4. Continue up the join. At the top, secure the threads and snip to neaten. Stitch the side and edges.

Lock stitch

This is also known as interlocking. It is used to lock the interlining to the face fabric when making interlined curtains, Roman shades, or pelmets.

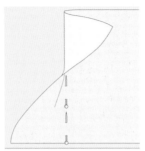

1. Place the fabric onto a flat surface wrong side uppermost. Lay the interlining onto the fabric and pin (vertically) through both layers.

2. Fold the interlining away from the edge. Make a couple of stitches in the interlining to secure and then, working downward toward the hem, take a couple of threads from the interlining and the fabric. Pull the needle through over the loose thread.

Project

Lock stitch is used on curtains, valances, and pelmets to secure the interlining.

Fabric

Lock stitch can be used on all fabrics. Inserting interlining adds body to thin fabrics and gives a luxurious finish to curtains. When using buckram on curtains for pinch pleat headings, lock stitch the interlining, starting 12 in. (30cm) from the top to allow the buckram to be inserted underneath.

Notions and stitch size

A medium to long needle is used and the stitches are 2–3 in. (5–7.5cm) long.

Alternative

There is no machine alternative for lock stitch.

Pressing and finishing

The project is not pressed at this stage.

3. Pull the thread to lock the stitch and continue to work toward the hem, making a stitch every 2–3 in. (5–7.5cm).

4. Do not pull the thread tight otherwise it will show on the front. Always use a thread that matches the face fabric.

5. Repeat these vertical stitching lines at 12 in. (30cm) intervals. The pins secure the interlining to the fabric until the lining is placed on top.

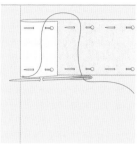

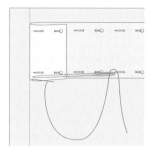

Herringbone stitch

Herringbone stitch secures two layers together. As it allows some movement, it can be used for hems. In curtain making it is used to sew buckram to the face fabric. The stitch is worked from left to right but the stitches themselves are worked from right to left.

1. Pin the buckram in position at the top of the curtain. Work from left to right at the bottom edge. Start by making a couple of stitches into the buckram. Work downward diagonally and take a few threads from the fabric from right to left ½ in. (1.2cm) along the fabric. Work upward diagonally to the right and make a stitch in the buckram from right to left, working in a parallel line to the buckram edge.

Project

Herringbone stitch is used to secure buckram and to join widths of interlining together. Overlap the layers by 1 in. (2.5cm) and make large stitches about 1 in. (2.5cm) apart through both layers. When using it as a hemming stitch, the folded edge will be facing. Take a larger stitch from the hem and a couple of threads from the fabric.

Fabric

Herringbone stitch is suitable for all fabrics.

Notions and stitch size

When sewing buckram, use a long medium-strength needle. The stitch size will vary from ½ in. (1.2cm) to 1 in. (2.5cm) depending on the thickness of the fabric and particular use.

Alternative

There is no machine alternative for sewing the buckram, but zigzag stitch could be used to sew the layers of interlining together.

Pressing and finishing

Press a hem lightly on the wrong side on a well-padded ironing board to prevent a ridge from forming.

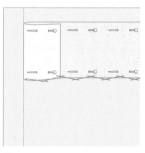

2. Continue to work across the width of the curtain, taking a couple of threads from the fabric and a larger stitch from the buckram. Secure to finish off.

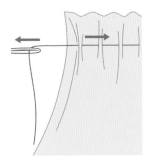

Gathering

To gather the fabric, use a running stitch pulled up to the required measurement. Small stitches will produce small gathers. Use larger stitches on thick fabric.

1. Secure the thread on the sewing line, and sew up and down through the fabric to create a row of even running stitches. For thicker fabrics it is a good idea to make another line of stitches ¼ in. (6mm) above the first line so the threads do not break when they are pulled up.

2. Pull the threads together to reduce the fabric to the desired length.

Project

Gathering is frequently used in home décor. It is used on bed skirts, pillowcases, and quilt covers, on frills around a pillow, as a trim on curtain valances and tiebacks, and on Austrian shades.

Fabric

Although most fabrics can be gathered, very thick fabrics are not suitable. Pleating is an alternative.

Notions and stitch size

Use a medium to long fine needle to make gathers quickly, as three or four stitches can be sewn at one time. Use double thread to add strength when making a single stitch line.

Alternative

Gathering is usually done on a sewing machine. Use the longest straight stitch available. Make two rows ¼ in. (6mm) apart.

Pressing and finishing

Do not press gathers as this will flatten them. Gathering threads can be removed if they are visible after the project is finished.

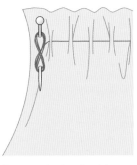

3. Secure the thread ends by securing around a vertical pin. Distribute the gathers evenly and sew as required.

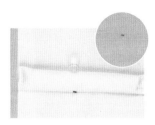

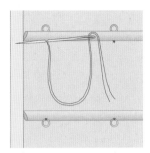

Stab stitch

This stitch secures layers of fabric together in one spot. It is used on a Roman shade to secure the lining to the face fabric, underneath the rod pockets.

1. Mark the positions where stab stitch is required (at the points where the cord rings are sewn onto the pockets).

2. Use a double thread of the face fabric color and make a knot in the end. Lift up the rod pocket, push the needle through all the thicknesses and, working toward the left, make a stitch ⅛ in. (3mm) long. Repeat this stitch five or six times to secure the layers.

Project

Stab stitch is mainly used to secure the layers together on a Roman shade.

Fabric

Use stab stitch on all types of fabric, taking care when interlining has been used to go through all the layers.

Notions and stitch size

It is best to use a long thin needle in this situation. Adjust the stitch length to accommodate the fabric thickness.

Alternative

There is no alternative machine stitch.

Pressing and finishing

No specific instructions are necessary.

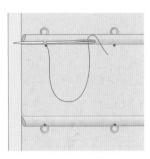

3. Make a couple of small stitches into the underneath layer of the rod pocket to finish off. Snip the threads. Repeat in all the appropriate places.

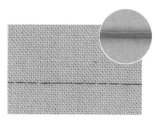

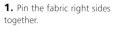

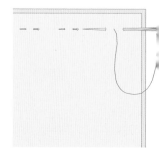

Back stitch

This can be used as an alternative to machine stitching.

1. Pin the fabric right sides together.

2. Working from right to left and having secured the thread on the wrong side, bring it through to the surface ¼ in. (6mm) from the starting point.

3. Take the needle down through the fabric ⅛ in. (3mm) back from this point and bring it back up to the surface the same distance in front of it.

4. Repeat this process so that with each stitch you insert the needle at the end of the previous stitch.

5. Continue to the end of the seam.

Project

Back stitch is an alternative to machine stitching short seams.

Fabric

Back stitch can be used on any fabric.

Notions and stitch size

Use a fine needle with cotton or polyester thread.

Alternative

Use a straight stitch on the sewing machine.

Pressing and finishing

Press the seam open with the pointed end of the iron.

Machine stitches

The stitches in this section are available on all modern machines. They are basic and functional, enabling seaming, finishing, and more decorative tasks to be carried out. The diagrams and examples will help you to set the machine correctly and sew the stitches required.

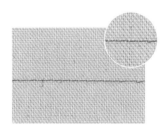

Straight stitch

Straight stitch is the original and most useful machine stitch available. It is very versatile and will allow most techniques to be undertaken—for example, seams, tucks, and gathering.

1. Check the sewing machine manual and set it up for straight stitching.

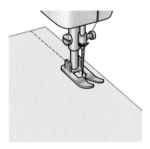

Project

Use straight stitch for everything from seaming to attaching trimmings, basting, and gathering.

Fabric

Straight stitch can be used on all types and weights of fabric, adjusting the stitch length if necessary.

Notions and stitch size

Use needles according to the type of fabric chosen (see pages 14–15). For fine fabric, use a short stitch of 16 stitches to 1 in. (1.5mm); for medium-weight fabric, use 10–12 stitches to 1 in. (2.5mm); for heavy or thick fabric, use a long stitch of 6–8 stitches to 1 in. (3mm).

2. Sew the seam in the position required, securing both ends by reversing the stitching for three or four stitches at the beginning and end of the machining.

Alternative

Use running stitch or back stitch when sewing by hand.

Pressing and finishing

No specific care is required.

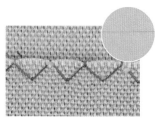

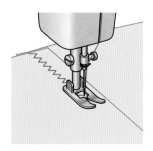

Zigzag stitch

Zigzag stitch is very versatile as the length and width of the stitches can be adjusted to suit different projects, such as neatening raw edges or stitching layers of interlining or batting together.

1. Set the machine to zigzag and adjust the length and width to suit the task. Check the machine manual as a guide and test the stitch on spare fabric first.

2. Place the fabric under the presser foot and, when overlapping a seam, zigzag over both layers.

Project

Use a wide zigzag for finishing edges and joining the interlining.

Fabric

Use zigzag stitch on all fabric types and weights, varying the length and width as necessary.

Notions and stitch size

Choose a needle to suit the fabric weight. The size of the zigzag will depend on the task.

Alternative

For neatening an edge, use an overcast stitch worked by hand or a serger (overlocker).

Pressing and finishing

No special instructions are necessary.

3. If neatening an edge, the needle will go right to the edge of the fabric.

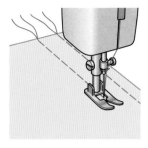

Gathering

Although gathering can be done by hand, it is much quicker on the sewing machine, particularly as there may be long lengths in home décor projects.

1. Set the sewing machine to the longest straight stitch or refer to the manual for instructions for gathering.

2. Before placing the fabric under the presser foot, make sure there is a tail of threads at least 3 in. (7.5cm) long. This makes pulling up the threads easier.

Project

Gathering is used to create frills on pillows, curtain valances, and bedding.

Fabric

Light- to mediumweight fabrics give the best results.

Notions and stitch size

Use size 11–14 depending on the fabric weight and set the stitch length at the longest straight stitch. You can alter the tension to allow the top thread to be pulled easily. Refer to the machine manual to follow these instructions.

Alternative

Hand gathering (page 48) can be used as an alternative.

Pressing and finishing

Do not press gathers as this will flatten them. When gathers are sewn in position, iron from the fullness of the fabric into the gathered folds with the pointed end of the iron.

3. Stitch a line of stitches just inside the seam allowance. (This ensures that the gathering stitches will not be on the actual sewing line when joining the gathered piece to the main item.) Sew a second line of stitching ¼ in. (6mm) parallel to the first. Leave a trail of threads and do not secure at either end.

4. Pull the top threads to draw up the gathering to the required measurement and wrap the threads around pins placed at the ends. Spread the gathers evenly and sew as required.

Seams and hems

There are many ways to join two pieces of fabric together, but it is important that you choose the correct one for the fabric you are using and for the desired outcome.

Plain seam

A plain seam is the easiest and most versatile method of joining two pieces of fabric together.

1. With right sides together, pin along the sewing line (at the required seam allowance).

2. Set the sewing machine to straight stitch and sew along this line, removing the pins in the process, or stitching over them carefully if necessary (see Pattern matching, page 41).

Project

Use a plain seam to join two pieces of fabric.

Fabric

A plain seam can be used on any fabric.

Notions and stitch size

Needle size and stitch length will depend on the fabric used.

Alternative

For long curtain seams there is not a practical hand-stitched alternative; for short lengths, use a back stitch.

Pressing and finishing

Press the seam open from the wrong side, using the pointed end of the iron to separate the edges. Turn the fabric over and lightly hover the iron over the seam, using a pressing cloth on delicate fabrics.

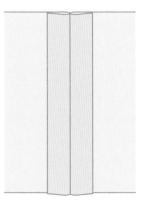

3. Press the seam open when completed.

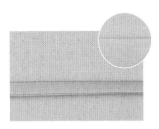

French seam

A French seam looks like a plain seam from the right side and a tuck from the wrong side. It is a neat way to finish a straight seam if a serger (overlocker) is not available.

1. With the wrong sides of the fabric together, pin and then machine ¼ in. (6mm) from the fabric edge with a straight stitch.

2. Trim the edge to ⅛ in. (3mm).

Project

Use when the reverse side of the article may be seen or when a serger is not available to neaten the seams.

Fabric

French seam is ideal for lightweight, sheer fabrics where the seam may be seen through the cloth.

Notions and stitch size

Use a fine needle (size 9 or 11), depending on the weight of the fabric.

3. Fold the seam the opposite way, so that right sides are together, and then pin ¼ in. (6mm) from the edge. Machine along this line, enclosing all the raw edges.

Alternative

Serge or zigzag any raw edges, but they will not be concealed.

Pressing and finishing

Press the seam to one side from the wrong side.

technique NOTE
When seams consist of several layers, it is advisable to graduate them for a smooth finish. Do this by cutting each seam allowance slightly longer than the one before.

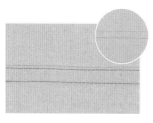

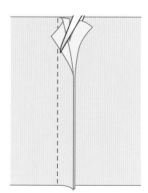

Flat fell seam

A flat fell seam has the seam allowance tucked under and sewn down with a second row of stitching. It is useful for unlined projects.

1. Place the wrong sides of the fabric together and sew ⅝ in. (16mm) from the edge.

2. Press the seam allowance to one side and trim the under-seam allowance to ⅛ in. (3mm).

Project

Use a flat fell seam for unlined projects as it is neat from both sides.

Fabric

A flat fell seam can be used on all but the heaviest fabrics, when a welt seam would be used as it does not fold under the seam allowance. However, it does leave a raw edge that will have to be neatened.

Notions and stitch size

Choose a needle and stitch length suitable for the fabric weight.

Alternative

A welt seam or plain seam with the seam allowance pressed to one side and top stitched will have a similar appearance.

Pressing and finishing

Press the fold with an iron and then press on completion.

3. Press the edge of the upper seam allowance under by ¼ in. (6mm). Edge stitch along the fold through all the layers to finish.

1. Cut a length of fabric 3 x 12 in. (8 x 30cm).

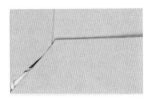

Lead weights

Lead weights are used to improve the hang of the curtains and are sewn into the hems. The round penny weights look like buttons with two holes and are available in different sizes for use with different fabric weights. They are sewn into the corners and on the seams of the curtains. After machining the fabric together, the seams can pucker slightly and even after snipping the selvage they can be tight. Sewing the weights in can help to smooth out the seams. Larger weights are used for heavier fabrics. When a light-colored fabric is used, the weights can be sewn into small pockets made from scraps of lining fabric.

2. Fold the fabric in half lengthwise. Open out and place the weight close to the center crease (with the holes parallel to the crease). Fold over the lining and using a zipper foot on a sewing machine (or back stitch by hand), stitch around the weight.

3. Repeat the process, leaving a gap of ½ in. (12mm) between each weight. Continue until enough weights are covered. Cut around each weight, leaving a ⅛ in. (3mm) seam allowance.

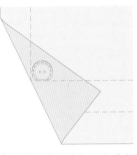

4. Hold up the weight to the light and it will be possible to see the holes. Turn the weight if necessary so the holes are parallel to the folded edge.

5. Sew on the weight as before through the holes with a double thread, positioning the edge of the lining fabric ⅛ in. (3mm) from the fold lines. This prevents a thick edge from forming on the fold of the fabric.

SHEER FABRICS

When working with sheer fabrics, you can use a lead weight in strip form. It is available by the yard (meter) in a stockinette tube and can be cut to any length. Lay it in the crease of the hem and attach it to the main fabric at regular intervals with a few stitches.

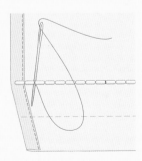

Cord pockets

Plastic cord tidies can be purchased to secure the cords from the heading tape, but cord pockets can be made from scraps of lining. They are sewn underneath the lower edge of the heading tape.

1. Cut a piece of lining fabric 6 x 5 in. (15 x 12.5cm).

2. Fold in half vertically and machine down the long side and across one short edge.

3. Turn inside out and press. Fold up 2 in. (5cm) to form a small pocket (on the finished end). Pin and then sew each side.

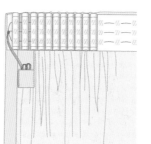

4. Position under the lower edge of the heading tape close to the outside edge of the curtain and sew in place when the tape is stitched on.

5. When the cords have been pulled up and tied in position, they can be placed into the pocket. (Do not cut the cords, as this would prevent the curtains from being stretched out for cleaning or washing.)

Miters

Miter the corners of curtain hems to distribute the fabric and prevent an untidy thick edge. Do this on all hems apart from unlined curtains with machined sides and hems.

1. Press the allowance at the sides (single fold) and then the hem of the curtain fabric (double fold).

2. Place a pin horizontally in the side fabric, where the hem meets the inner edge of the side fold.

3. Starting with the left side of the curtain, open out the fabric completely and fold from the pin, through the corner (the miter point) to the bottom edge of the hem and smooth down.

Front

4. Holding the side edge with your left hand, use your right hand to fold up the first layer.

5. Then fold up the second layer, keeping the fabric as smooth as possible.

Reverse

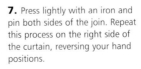

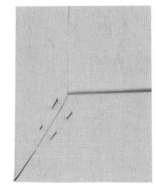

7. Press lightly with an iron and pin both sides of the join. Repeat this process on the right side of the curtain, reversing your hand positions.

8. Sew the weights in the corner (see page 57) and use ladder stitch (see page 45) to complete the process.

6. Fold in the side edge and press with your fingers so that the angled edges come together.

Window treatments

This section explains in detail the methods used to create many different home décor projects for decorating your windows. It covers not only many styles of curtains and Roman shades, but also valances, tiebacks, and pelmets, all of which help to create a personalized look for your home style.

Curtains

Choosing the best curtain length and heading style for your window type is important and will determine how much fabric you need.

Measuring windows

When measuring a window, use a metal retractable tape measure as it will give more accurate measurements. It is much easier to take these measurements when the track or pole has already been fitted. However, if that is not possible, you can estimate the measurements to get an idea of the amount of fabric required. This will give you the opportunity to work out the cost of a particular fabric and you can alter your design or fabric choice to suit your budget.

Width

For the width, measure the required width including the stackback (the amount of fabric that will sit at the side of the window). Allow 2–2½ in. (5–6cm) for the overlap in the center and for ease. It is much better to be generous with the fabric, rather than struggling to keep the center together if the heading is tight. (On corded tracks the overlap arm length may differ, so it is sensible to check this measurement.)

Length

If using a track, measure from the top of the track to the finished length. To establish the hook position on a track, measure from the top of the track to the center of the glider. This will be the hook position on the heading tape, so you can position the tape accordingly.

If you are using a curtain pole, measure from the bottom of the ring to the finished length (see opposite). This will be the hook position, so add ½ in. (1cm) to the length of the curtain to cover it.

Curtain type

For eyelet curtains, measure from the top of the pole to the required length and add 1 in. (2.5cm).

For tab top curtains, measure from the top of the pole to the required length. The length of the tabs is included in this measurement (see page 72). The pole must be high enough above the window so that light does not come through between the tabs.

measurements NOTE
For full-length curtains, it is a good idea to take measurements at each end and at the center of the window to check that the floor is even. Adjustments to the curtain length can be made during construction. This is done by folding over a little more on one side to achieve the correct measurement when putting on heading tape or inserting buckram.

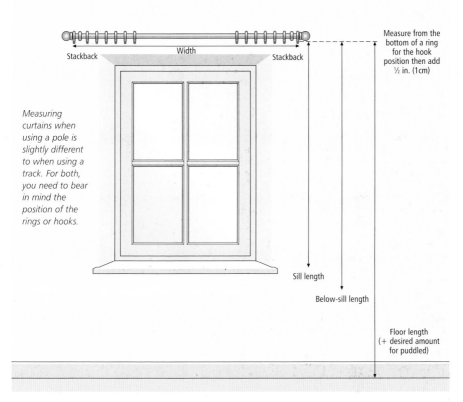

Measuring curtains when using a pole is slightly different to when using a track. For both, you need to bear in mind the position of the rings or hooks.

Stackback

Width

Stackback

Measure from the bottom of a ring for the hook position then add ½ in. (1cm)

Sill length

Below-sill length

Floor length (+ desired amount for puddled)

Checklist for curtains

Copy this checklist, fill it in, and take it with you to the fabric store.

FABRIC

Design _____

Color _____

LINING

Lined ☐
Unlined ☐
Interlined ☐

HEADING STYLE

Pinch/triple pleat ☐
Pencil pleat ☐
Tab tops ☐
Goblet pleat ☐
Inverted pleat ☐
Box pleat ☐
Eyelet ☐

Heading height _____

CURTAIN LENGTH

Track/pole to sill ☐
Track/pole to below sill ☐
Track/pole to floor ☐
Puddled ☐

Curtain length _____

ACCESSORIES

Valance ☐
Pelmet ☐
Tiebacks ☐
Trim ☐

What works where

Many things need to be taken into consideration when deciding on a window treatment: the selection of the correct fabric so that the curtain will perform the function you want; the style you choose so that it will enhance the rest of the décor and furnishings; and your ability to produce a professional finish that you will be proud of.

• **Full-length curtains** are the most attractive to show off a beautiful fabric and a feature window, but this is not always possible or practical. A layer of interlining can add bulk and glamor to curtains, and sometimes it is possible to use fewer widths of fabric this way.

• **Lining curtains** is important to protect the fabric from sun damage, to add warmth and to produce a professional, neat finish.

• **Unlined curtains** are useful in kitchens and bathrooms, where they will need laundering frequently. They can also give a floaty, translucent appearance and look attractive when combined with shades.

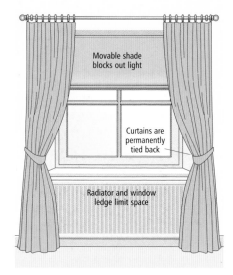

Movable shade blocks out light

Curtains are permanently tied back

Radiator and window ledge limit space

• **When space is limited**—for example, a radiator or deep window ledge—there is often a way to work around this situation. Full-length curtains can be permanently tied back at the sides and a shade can be used to cover the glass. These curtains will not pull across, so do not need to have several widths. They can be as narrow as 1½ widths each side. Interlining these curtains is ideal and will add a touch of luxury to this type of window dressing.

• **When the window is close to a wall,** just one curtain can be draped toward the wider side. This method also works when a narrow window requires curtains. It often looks better to have just one curtain pulled to one side.

design NOTE
For more window designs and treatments, see the Design directory on pages 196–209.

Positioning

It is important to maximize the impact of the window, which is often the focal point in a room. By positioning carefully, the illusion of extra height and width can be created.

• **To increase the width of a narrow window,** extend the track or pole either side so the open curtains just cover the edge of the window. The amount of wall that is covered by the track or pole is called the stackback.

• **To make a wide window look narrower,** reduce the width of the track, so that more of the window is covered when the curtains are open. This is only sensible when blocking out sunlight is not an issue.

• **To lower the height of a tall window,** place a deep valance or pelmet across the top, covering some of the glass.

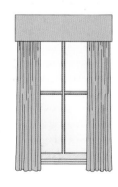

• **To raise the height of a low window,** place the valance or pelmet high above the window, so that the lower edge just covers the top of the window.

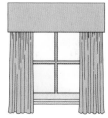

Calculating fabric in 5 easy steps

Different styles of curtain will require different amounts of fabric. All curtains are made up of widths of fabric that are gathered in some way to cover a window when drawn across. When they are open, they will hang according to the type of heading and the quantity of fabric used.

Here are a few rules to follow that will give you the best results:

1 **Decide on heading**
Once you have chosen the desired heading style and the finished length, it is possible to calculate the amount of fabric required.

HEADING TYPE	FABRIC REQUIREMENTS
Simple narrow gathering tape	2 times width
Pencil pleat tape	2¼–2½ times
Tab top	1½ times
Pinch pleat	2–2¼ times
Eyelet	1½ times
Goblet	2–2¼ times
Inverted	2–2¼ times
Box	2½–3 times
Sheer	2½–3 times

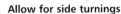

measurements NOTE
It is sensible to round up to the next whole yard (meter) as any extra fabric can be used for cushions or tiebacks.

2 **Allow for side turnings**
These are about 2 in. (5cm) but only need to be taken into consideration when pinch pleating or other fixed heading is used. It may be necessary to add an extra width of fabric (half a width each side) when the measurements are on the borderline of increasing the number of widths.

3 Allow for hem allowances
These are usually 10 in. (25cm). This allows 8 in. (20cm) at the hem and 2 in. (5cm) at the top. This can be reduced to accommodate a pattern repeat, but it would not be good to reduce it to as little as 5 in. (12.5cm), as this would make the hem flimsy. On short curtains it is only necessary to allow a 6 in. (15cm) hem.

4 Multiply the finished width by the heading requirement
This amount is then divided by the fabric width (usually 54 in. [137cm]) to calculate the number of widths required. Multiply this number by the length (including hem allowances) to achieve the total amount required. The pattern repeat also has to be taken into consideration (see page 39). For example:

Track width for a pair of pencil pleat headed curtains is 100 in. (250cm).
Length of curtains is 80 in. (200cm).
Pattern repeat on the fabric is 25 in. (64cm).
100 in. (250cm) x 2½ times = 250 in. (635cm).
250 in. (635cm) ÷ 54 in. (137cm) = 4⅗ (4.6) rounded up to 5 widths (2½ widths each side).
Length is 80 in. (200cm) + 10 in. (25cm) (hem allowance) = 90 in. (228cm). This is rounded up to 100 in. (254cm) to accommodate the pattern repeat (25 in. [64cm] x 4).
Therefore, 5 x 100 in. (250cm) = 500 in. (1,270cm) = 13⅞ yd (10.24m).

5 Before cutting
It is a good idea to measure the required number of lengths and mark with a pin in the selvage to confirm that enough fabric has been purchased. It may be possible to reduce the hem allowance slightly if necessary.

Calculating lining
This is much easier to work out. The pattern repeat does not have to be taken into consideration and the hem allowance is 6 in. (15cm) for curtains with heading tape and 10 in. (25cm) for curtains with hand-stitched pinch pleat or goblet heading where the lining reaches to the top of the fabric.

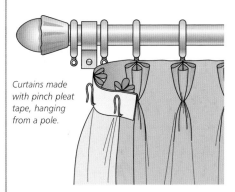

Curtains made with pinch pleat tape, hanging from a pole.

Using narrow heading tape can help produce a ruffle so that the track can be covered.

Unlined curtains

There are circumstances where unlined curtains are appropriate, for example, in bathrooms and kitchens because they are easy to care for. Soft floral curtains look attractive when accompanying Roman or roller shades. The opacity is the attraction, allowing sunlight to stream through, but with little insulation.

SKILL LEVEL
• 1

TOOLS
• Scissors
• Soft tape measure
• Metal tape measure
• Sewing kit

MATERIALS
• Fabric
• Thread
• Lead weights
• Heading tape
• Curtain pole or track
• Curtain hooks

SEE ALSO
• Curtains, p62
• Fabric characteristics, p38
• Hand stitches, p42
• Machine stitches, p51
• Seams and hems, p54

Cords are tucked into the first pleat or behind the hook to secure.

1. Measure the window and calculate the amount of fabric you will need (see pages 62–67). Cut the fabric with care, making sure it is square. Pulling a thread may be useful or following a printed pattern from selvage to selvage (see page 38). Mark the top front side of each piece with a pin or tailor's chalk. ▼

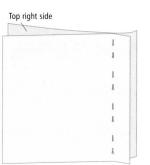

Top right side

2. If you are using plain fabric, place the widths right sides together to join and pin from the bottom edge upward, allowing 1 in. (2.5cm) seam allowance. It may be necessary to trim off the selvage (if it is tight) and then use a flat fell seam or French seam (see pages 54–56).

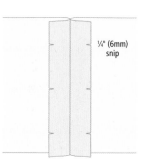

¼" (6mm) snip

3. Machine stitch, snip the selvage every 6 in. (15cm), and press the seam open. If you are using a patterned fabric, the pattern must be matched across all the widths (see page 41).

1" (2.5cm)

4. At the side edges, cut off the selvage and press in 2 in. (5cm). Turn under 1 in. (2.5cm) and pin close to the edge. Machine both sides close to the edge.

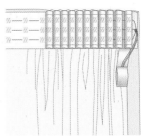

5. Press up 6 in. (15cm) at the hem. Turn under 3 in. (7.5cm) (fold hem in half). Pin and machine stitch close to the edge. Leave 12 in. (30cm) of thread at each end to finish off the corners by hand. ▼

3" (7.5cm)

Exact finished length

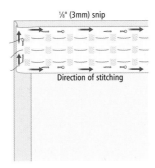

⅛" (3mm) snip

Direction of stitching

7. Press the curtains. Tie the cords together at the inside edge and pull the cords at the outside edge to the required length—half the track width plus 2–3 in. (5–8cm) (so that the curtains meet in the middle). Do not cut the cords off, as the curtains cannot be stretched out again for cleaning. A plastic or card cord tidy can be used to wind the cords around, or a pocket can be made from lining and sewn under the lower stitching line on the heading tape (see page 58). Insert plastic or metal curtain hooks every 2–3 in. (5–8cm) into the pockets on the tape and hang onto the track or pole, securing the outside edge.

6. Place on to a flat surface, wrong side up. Measure and mark the finished length with a line of pins. Fold over and pin the top, trimming off any excess fabric to 2¼ in. (6cm). Pin the heading tape on, tucking in the ends and securing the raw edges. Machine stitch, as shown in the diagram, to avoid twisting the tape. Do not stitch over the cords at the ends of the heading tape as these will be knotted at the inside edge and used to pull up to the exact finished width. Finish off the ends and remove all the pins.

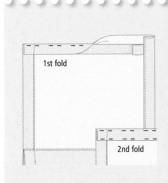

1st fold

2nd fold

technical NOTE
If pinch pleat heading is required, sew in buckram (see pages 82–83). To conceal it, add twice the length. Pin the buckram above the finished marked length and fold over the top fabric twice. Fold the end to the side edge hem. Slip stitch the ends and make the pleats following instructions for Triple pleat (see pages 84–86).

Lined curtains

Lining curtains is important as it protects the fabric from sun damage and gives greater sound and heat insulation. It also produces a more professional and neater finish.

SKILL LEVEL
• 1

TOOLS
• Scissors
• Soft tape measure
• Metal tape measure
• Sewing kit

MATERIALS
• Fabric
• Lining
• Thread
• Lead weights
• Heading tape
• Curtain pole or track
• Curtain hooks

SEE ALSO
• Curtains, p62
• Fabric characteristics, p38
• Hand stitches, p42
• Machine stitches, p51
• Seams and hems, p54
• Unlined curtains, p68

1. Measure the window and calculate the amount of fabric you will need (see pages 62–67). Cut the fabric, taking care that it is square (see page 38). When cutting fabric with a printed pattern, follow the pattern and not the grain, so the pattern will appear as continuous when the curtains are hanging. Mark the top front side of each width with a pin or tailor's chalk.

2. If more than one width is required, the pattern needs to match at the side edges. Take two pieces of fabric right sides and edges together. The easiest way to join an obvious pattern is to fold back the top layer to see where the corresponding pattern appears. Crease the fold line with your fingers and replace. Pin through the crease line. Repeat every few inches and pin the fabric together in between. A straight line will form. Sometimes with a patterned fabric the two edges do not come together because there is more selvage on one side. This is not a problem and it is possible to keep this distance all the way to the top. Start from the bottom and work upward.

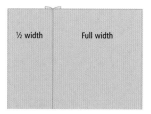

½ width   Full width

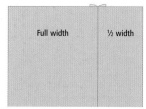

Full width   ½ width

3. When an odd number of fabric widths is required, stitch a half width to the outside edges. If there are only a few widths to join, stitch them all together first and then cut up through the center of the middle width, so that half a width can be placed on the outside edge.

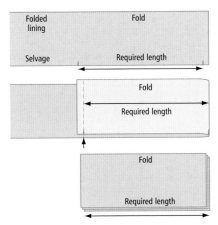

4. If you are using a horizontal stripe, check, or geometric pattern, pin the fabric together at right angles to the edge. This keeps the pattern match correct and stops the fabric stretching. The pins can be machine stitched over. It may be necessary to use pins in both directions. Press the seams open. Snip the selvage every 6 in. (15cm) to take away any tightening. Check that the pattern matches. You may need to unpick and restitch small sections. If the selvage or seam allowance is more than 2 in. (5cm) it can be trimmed off, as it may be bulky. ➤

6. Pin the widths together with the lining lying flat on the table, starting from the bottom edge. Use 1 in. (2.5cm) seam allowance. Machine stitch the lining. Snip the selvages every 6 in. (15cm) and press the seams open. ➤

5. To cut the lengths of folded lining, place the lining onto a flat surface with the selvage closest to you and the cut edge on the right. Snip into the selvage a few inches or centimeters from the cut edge. Measure the exact length required and make another snip. Fold the first part of the lining over to the left (back on itself), matching up the selvage and folded edge. Smooth the fabric and cut through the folded edge. This will be 90 degrees and perfectly square (bottom edge). Measure the required length from this cut edge and cut through all the layers. Cut as many lengths as required by layering the lining. ➤

7. Press up 6 in. (15cm) at the hem and then turn under 3 in. (7.5cm) (fold in half). Pin and then machine stitch close to the top edge (the sides of the lining will be turned in when it is placed onto the curtain fabric). ◀

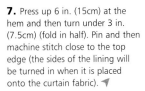

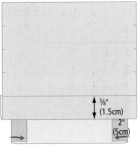

8. To establish how much face fabric to turn in at the side, for a single width, lay the fabric wrong side up on a flat surface and place the lining on top. Fold in the sides of the fabric (for standard width fabrics and lining the fold-in will be approximately 2 in. [5cm]) until the lining hangs over the edge by ⅝ in. (1.5cm).

If you are using two widths, match the seams of the fabric and lining, and spread out toward the edges. Turn in the sides as before. Pin and trim to 2 in. (5cm) if necessary. Snip the selvage every 6 in. (15cm), but not the bottom 16 in. (40cm). Press the side edges. ↘

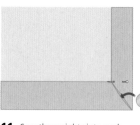

9. Fold up the hem 8 in. (20cm), following the pattern all the way across the widths, then press. Turn under 4 in. (10cm) (fold in half) and press again. (By doing it this way, it is necessary only to measure once; the second procedure is a fold.) ➤

10. To make the miter corners, place a pin horizontally on the side edge where the hem cuts across, then follow the instructions for Miters on page 59. Mitering the corner enables you to keep all the fabric without causing a bulky thick edge. It may be necessary at a later date to lengthen the curtain. ➤

11. Sew the weights into each bottom corner and at every seam: open out the corner of the fabric and place a weight ⅛ in. (3mm) from each crease, and with double thread sew it on like a button (see page 57). If using a light-colored or lightweight fabric, you can make a pocket for the weight from lining fabric. Stitch up the corner using a ladder stitch (see page 45), bringing the fabric together. ▼

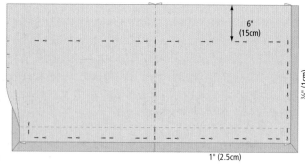

6"
(15cm)

⅜" (1cm)

1" (2.5cm)

12. Stitch the curtain all around, starting at the top right-hand side, using a slip stitch and a slip hemming stitch along the bottom edge (see pages 42–43), and then up to the top left-hand side. ➤

13. To put the lining on, lay the curtain wrong side up onto a flat surface. Place the lining on top, lining right side up, matching the seams where necessary. Pin the bottom edge of the lining 1 in. (2.5cm) up from the curtain edge and along the center seams where appropriate. At the sides, snip the selvage of the lining and turn under the edge to allow ⅜ in. (1cm) of curtain fabric to show. Pin the sides and along the top edge 6 in. (15cm) from the top. (See diagram above.) ➤

14. Stitch the lining using a slip stitch (see page 42) with lining-colored thread, making sure that the stitches don't come through to the front. At the hem edge, stitch 1½ in. (4cm) along the bottom from each corner, leaving the rest of the bottom edge loose. Also stitch 1½ in. (4cm) either side of the seams to secure. Don't remove the pins at the edges at this stage, as they keep the layers together.

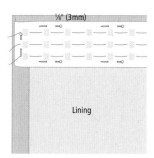

⅛" (3mm)

Lining

Lining

Lining

15. To attach the heading tape, place the curtain on a flat surface, lining side uppermost. Using a metal tape measure, measure from the bottom edge to the required length and fold over any excess. Pin to secure and trim to 2¼–2½ in. (6cm) for standard 3 in. (7.5cm) deep heading tape.

16. Place the heading tape ⅛ in. (3mm) from the top, overlapping 1½ in. (4cm) at the sides. Position the hook pocket ½ in. (1cm) to the side hem of the leading (inside) edge. Pin the top and bottom, and tuck under the corners of fabric. Fold the heading tape under the corner to conceal all the raw ends. Pull the cords out so they are not stitched.

17. Machine stitch in the direction shown in the diagram, starting at the bottom left-hand side. Finish off the ends securely and remove all the pins. You can make a pocket for the cords and insert it into the lower stitching line (see page 58).

18. To finish, make sure all the threads and pins are removed. Press the curtains, starting with the lining side. Steam is usually required. Do not press the heading tape. Press the right side from the top downward.

19. Tie the cords at the inside edge. Pull the cords from the outside edge to the correct width plus a couple of inches or a few centimeters to make sure that the curtains meet in the middle. Use a cord tidy or make a small pocket from lining to ensure that the cords don't get tangled. Don't cut off the cords, as the curtain then cannot be stretched out for cleaning. (See Unlined curtains, pages 68–69 for tips on hanging.)

Lining the curtain gives a more substantial finish.

Tab top curtains

Tab top curtains are informal and are often unlined. They can be used along with shades, to dress the side of the window. They do not pull back smoothly so are ideal as dress curtains that are not drawn daily.

Tab top curtains require 1½ times the window width. Use a pole to slot through the tabs and place it 4 in. (10cm) above the window. When calculating the amount of fabric, measure from above the window opening or architrave. Measure the tab length around the pole from the top edge of the curtain, approximately 7 in. (17.5cm). The tab width can be up to 2 in. (5cm) wide.

Unlined tab tops

Lightweight fabrics are perfect for unlined tab tops.

SKILL LEVEL
• 1

TOOLS
• Scissors
• Soft tape measure
• Metal tape measure
• Sewing kit

MATERIALS
• Fabric
• Thread
• Pole

SEE ALSO
• Curtains, p62
• Fabric characteristics, p38
• Unlined curtains, p68
• Hand stitches, p42
• Machine stitches, p51
• Seams and hems, p54
• Tiebacks, p92

1. Cut the fabric, allowing 10 in. (25cm) for the turnings. Follow steps 2–4 for Unlined curtains (see page 68), pressing up 8 in. (20cm) at the hem. Fold under 4 in. (10cm) and machine across the hem, leaving 12 in. (30cm) of thread at each end to finish the corners by hand.

3. Fold the tab strip in half vertically, right sides together, and stitch on the sewing machine with ½ in. (1.3cm) seam allowance. Press the seam open and turn through to the right side. You may need to attach a seam tape to the end and pull it through, as in the Braided tieback (see page 94). Press again and position the seam in the center. Cut into 8 in. (20cm) sections and fold in half horizontally.

2. Decide on the tab width then double it and add 1¼ in. (3cm) seam allowance. Add 1¼ in. (3cm) allowance to the tab length. For a 2 x 7 in. (5 x 17.5cm) tab, cut strips of 5¼ x 8¼ in. (13 x 21cm). It may be possible to cut several tabs together if a suitable piece of fabric is available, e.g. fabric length = 33 in. (84cm), therefore a strip 5¼ x 33 in. (13 x 84cm) will produce four tabs.

design NOTE
When cutting the tabs, use the fabric pattern to make a feature of the design if possible. If you cut the tabs randomly, organize them when they are placed on top of the curtain.

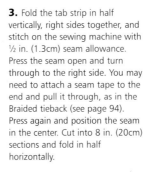

4. Lay the curtain onto a flat surface, right side upward. Measure the length required, adding the tab length to the top, and trim off any excess to leave ⅝ in. (1.5cm) seam allowance. Position the tabs along the top edge. Place one at each end and leave a 4 in. (10cm) gap between each tab. This can be adjusted if necessary. Pin and machine, taking ½ in. (1.3cm) seam allowance. Stitch across the tabs twice.

7. Fold over the facing and press downward. Turn under ⅜ in. (1cm) and pin along the bottom edge of the facing. Stitch the bottom and side edges.

5. Cut a facing strip, the width of the curtain plus 2 in. (5cm) for the seam allowance by 3 in. (7.5cm) wide.

6. With right sides together, pin the facing strip onto the curtain, pinning from the wrong side so that the tab stitching line is visible. Fold in the side seam allowances and stitch across all the layers.

Using a tab top heading with this material maximizes the impact of the stripes.

8. Press and slot the tabs onto the pole, leaving one tab to the outside of the support fixing.

Lined tab tops

Lining tab tops will provide greater insulation.

Lined tab tops with facing

Facing adds structure to lightweight fabric, improving the hang of the curtains. The lower stitching line of the facing encloses all the raw edges of a fabric that might otherwise ravel easily.

1. Follow the instructions for Lined curtains, steps 1–14 (see pages 70–71).

2. Follow the instructions for Unlined tab tops, steps 4–8 (see page 75), to complete the curtains. On step 6, graduate the seam allowance before folding over the facing, as it can become bulky (see note on page 55).

Lined tab tops without facing

There is an alternative method of completing lined tab tops that avoids adding a facing and does not leave any machine stitching visible. To use this method follow the instructions below.

1. Follow steps 1–12 for Lined curtains (see pages 70–72).

2. Stitch the curtain all around using a slip stitch at the side and a slip hemming stitch (see pages 42–43) along the bottom edge. Do not stitch the top 12 in. (30cm) on the side edges.

Lining without facing produces a smooth finish with no stitching lines showing.

3. Lay the curtain onto a flat surface, right side facing upward, and measure the length required, adding the tab length at the top (total length) and trim off any excess to leave ⅝ in. (1.5cm) seam allowance. Open out the side edges and position the tabs along the top. Place one at each end and leave 4 in. (10cm) gaps between the tabs. Adjust if necessary.

4. Machine stitch twice across the tabs, taking ½ in. (1.3cm) seam allowance. ▼

5. Trim the lining ⅝ in. (1.5cm) less than the finished curtain length (not including the tabs). ▼

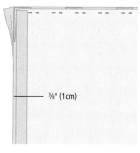

⅜" (1cm)

6. With right sides together, pin the lining to the top edge, just below the stitching line of the tabs. Start from the center of the curtain and work outward. At the sides, fold the lining edge to the wrong side to reveal ⅜ in. (1cm) of fabric. Fold over the side of the main fabric. Pin and machine stitch across the top through all thicknesses just below the tab stitching line.

7. Trim off the corners and graduate the seam allowance (see note on page 55). ▼

8. Complete the stitching at the top of the side edges left unfinished at step 2. Turn the lining to the wrong side and smooth downward. Pin the sides of the lining to the fabric, snipping the selvage of the lining if necessary, revealing ⅜ in. (1cm). The lining will reach to within 1 in. (2.5cm) of the bottom edge.

9. Stitch the side edges and at the hem edge, stitch 1½ in. (4cm) from each corner using a slip stitch. ▼

10. Press and slot onto the pole, leaving one tab to the outside of the support fixing.

Interlined curtains

Adding a layer of interlining between the fabric and lining produces a luxurious effect to curtains. There are various weights and thicknesses of interlining, some easier to handle than others. Interlining will add significantly to the weight of the curtains, particularly if they are full-length, so a sturdy pole or track will be required. The folds on curtains hang beautifully with interlining, and do not crease as much when tied back, so the extra effort is well worth it.

SKILL LEVEL
- 2

TOOLS
- Scissors
- Soft tape measure
- Metal tape measure
- Sewing kit
- Table clamps or weights
- Lead weights

MATERIALS
- Fabric
- Lining
- Interlining
- Thread
- Heading tape
- Curtain track or pole
- Curtain hooks

SEE ALSO
- Lined curtains, p70
- Fabric characteristics, p38
- Hand stitches, p42
- Machine stitches, p51
- Seams and hems, p54

1. Cut the fabric and lining as for making Lined curtains (see page 70).

2. To cut the interlining, check that the cut edge is square (see Fabric characteristics, page 38) and measure the required length. This will be 10 in. (25cm) longer than the finished length. Cut the required lengths. Pin the widths together, overlapping the edges by ¾ in. (2cm), starting from the bottom edge and working upward. Use a zigzag stitch (see page 52). Snip the selvages as these may be more tightly woven.

3. Follow the instructions for Lined curtains, steps 2–11 (see pages 70–72) to join the fabric widths together and prepare the lining. Press the side edges and hem on the fabric before sewing on the interlining as this will simplify future processes.

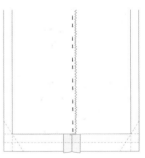

4. Place the fabric wrong side facing upward onto a flat surface. Use table clamps or weights to stop the fabric slipping and to make sure that it is square. Use the side and end edges of the table to align the fabric. Open out the side and hem the edges, and then place the interlining on top. Match up the seams (the first leading, inside edge seam when using more than two widths of fabric) or fabric and interlining, and pin through all the layers. The bottom edge of the interlining will be placed on the hem line crease.

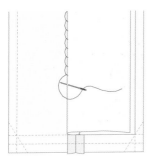

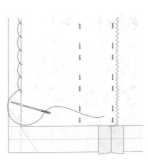

5. Fold the interlining over to expose the seam. Using a lock stitch (see page 46), interlock the interlining to the fabric, picking up small stitches on the fabric. Always use the main fabric-colored thread in case any small stitches show through on the front.

6. Fold the interlining across the fabric again and, 12 in. (30cm) to the left of the first stitching line, pin vertically through both layers. Fold the interlining to the right and interlock along this line. Repeat this process to the edge.

7. Cut the interlining into the fold line of the side edge and interlock into the crease. Return to the center and repeat the sequence to the other side edge. Trim the interlining at the hem edge if necessary, and pin the sides and hem.

8. Stitch lead weights into the corners and on each seam of the hem (see page 57), and ladder stitch the miters (see page 45). Using a slip and slip hemming stitch (see pages 42–43), stitch all around the curtain.

9. To place the lining onto the fabric, follow the instructions in step 14 of Lined curtains (see page 72).

10. When marking the exact finished length, the interlining is trimmed on this line, so it is not bulky underneath the heading tape.

11. For finishing tips, follow the instructions for Lined curtains, steps 15–16 (see page 73).

As with lined curtains, the pencil pleat tape works well.

Interlined curtains with triple pleat heading

When making interlined curtains with a triple or pinch pleat heading, buckram is sewn at the top, underneath the interlining (see Other headings, page 82). The interlining is stitched onto the fabric up to 10 in. (25cm) from the top. It is folded back and the buckram is placed up to the line marking the finished length. This method can be used also for making goblet, inverted, or box pleats.

SKILL LEVEL
• 3

ADDED REQUIREMENTS
• Buckram (instead of heading tape)
• Craft pins
• Pin hooks

SEE ALSO
• Interlined curtains, p78
• Lined valance, p96
• Other headings, p80

1. Pin the buckram along the top and bottom edges, using craft pins (as they are strong enough to pierce through buckram) and overlapping the edges of the curtains by 5 in. (12.5cm). Fold in the buckram on the side edge crease line. The double thickness provides extra strength when the pin hooks are inserted at the edges.

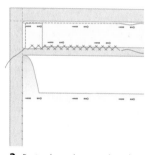

2. Baste along the top edge of the buckram and herringbone stitch the bottom edge (see pages 44 and 47).

3. Take out the pins and replace the folded interlining. Smooth upward and trim to within ¼ in. (6mm) of the top of the buckram.

design NOTE
The finished sample (far right) shows how a button can be used as a decorative detail on each pleat. Cover the button with the curtain fabric for a slick finish or add an accent of color by using a contrasting fabric.

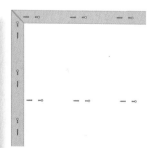

4. Fold the top edge of the fabric over the buckram and interlining, remembering to take out the pins that marked the finished length. Pin with craft pins through all the layers. Miter the corners as in step 3 for the Lined valance (see page 96), and ladder stitch to close.

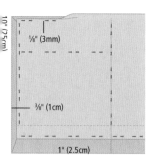

10" (25cm)

⅛" (3mm)

⅜" (1cm)

1" (2.5cm)

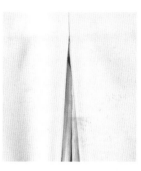

8. To calculate the pleat positions and complete the curtains, see pages 84–87.

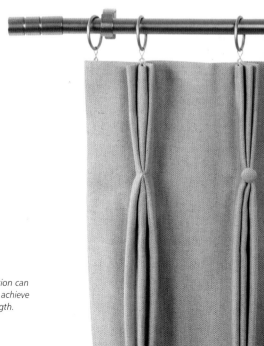

The back of the curtain is as neatly finished as the front.

5. Place the fabric onto a flat surface, wrong side uppermost, and place the lining on top, right side uppermost, matching the seams where necessary. Pin the bottom edge of the lining 1 in. (2.5cm) up from the bottom edge. At the side edges, snip the selvage of the lining and turn under to allow ⅜ in. (1cm) of curtain fabric to show. It may be necessary to trim off any excess lining if it extends more than 1¼ in. (3cm). ▼

6. Smooth the lining up to the top edge and fold under the edge to allow ⅛ in. (3mm) of fabric to show. Trim the excess lining if there is more than 2 in. (5cm). Place a line of pins about 10 in. (25cm) from the top of the curtains, to hold the layers in place until the pleats are made.

7. Stitch the lining to the side hem using a slip stitch. At the hem edge, stitch 1½ in. (4cm) from each corner along the bottom, leaving the rest of the bottom edge loose. At the seams stitch 1½ in. (4cm) either side, or make a loop chain to secure. Do not take out the pins from the top and bottom edges at this stage.

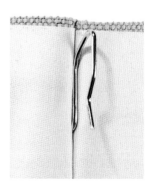

The hook position can be adjusted to achieve the correct length.

Other headings

There are a variety of different headings for curtains that all start off with the same process. This process consists of sewing buckram onto the top of the fabric, enclosing all the raw edges with lining and then forming a variety of different pleats to create a stylish, elegant effect. The curtains look best hanging from a pole and pulled back neatly to reveal the maximum amount of light in the room.

SKILL LEVEL
• 3

TOOLS
• Scissors
• Soft tape measure
• Metal tape measure
• Sewing kit
• Craft pins

MATERIALS
• Fabric
• Lining
• Thread
• Lead weights
• Buckram
• Pin hooks

SEE ALSO
• Lined curtains, p70
• Hand stitches, p42
• Lined valance, p96

1. Follow the instructions for Lined curtains, steps 1–12 (see pages 70–72).

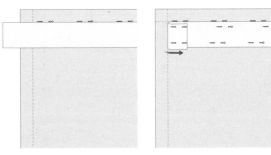

2. Place the curtain, wrong side uppermost onto a flat surface, using the side edges of the table to keep the fabric square. Measure to the finished length and mark with a line of pins. Place the top edge of the buckram on this line, overlapping the side edges by 5 in. (12.5cm). Pin the buckram to the fabric along the top and bottom edges, using craft pins and keeping the fabric smooth. At the side edges, fold over the buckram on the side edge crease line to give a double layer (this provides a strong edge for inserting the pin hooks).

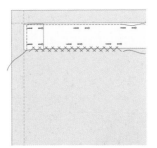

3. Baste along the top edge (see page 44). The bottom edge is stitched with a herringbone stitch (see page 47).

4. Fold the top edge of the fabric over the buckram and transfer the pins from the buckram through both layers. Miter the corners as in step 3 of Lined valance (see page 96) and ladder stitch (see page 45) to close. Take out the pins from the bottom edge of the buckram. Stitch the curtain all around, as explained in step 14 on page 72. ▼

⅛"
(3mm)

1" (2.5cm)

5. Replace the fabric onto a flat surface wrong side uppermost and place the lining on top, right side uppermost, matching the seams where necessary. Pin the bottom edge of the lining 1 in. (2.5cm) up from the curtain edge and up the seams, where necessary. At the side edges, snip the selvage of the lining and turn under to allow ⅜ in. (1cm) of curtain fabric to show. It may be necessary to trim off any excess lining if it extends more than 1¼ in. (3cm). Smooth the lining up to the top and fold under the edge to allow ⅛ in. (3mm) of fabric to show. Trim any excess lining if there is more than 2 in. (5cm). Place a line of pins about 10 in. (25cm) from the top of the curtain as this will hold everything in place until the pleats are made.

6. Stitch the lining to the side hem using a slip stitch (see page 42) with lining-colored thread, making sure that the stitching does not appear on the front of the curtain. At the hem edge stitch 1½ in. (4cm) along the bottom from each corner, leaving the rest of the bottom edge loose. At the seams stitch 1½ in. (4cm) either side. Do not remove the pins at the bottom and top edges.

Position the hook away from the edge to allow the curtains to overlap.

7. At this stage it is possible to create several different headings (see below).

Triple (French) pleats
page 84

Goblet pleats
page 87

Inverted pleats
page 87

Box pleats
page 87

Eyelet heading
page 88

Puffed heading
page 89

Triple (French) pleats

There are usually 4–5 pleats per width of curtaining and the optimum size for the pleats is 6–8 in. (15–20cm).

Measure the width of the finished curtain and subtract the track width from it. For example, if the track/pole width is 92 in. (234cm), then half of this width is 46 in. (117cm). Allow a 4 in. (10cm) tolerance and the desired finished width is 50 in. (127cm).

The finished curtain measures 104 in. (262cm). Therefore, 104 – 50 in. (262 – 127cm) = 54 in. (135cm). This will be the amount of fabric available for the pleats.

So, 54 ÷ 6 in. (135 ÷ 15cm) for each pleat = 9 pleats. There are eight gaps and two ends. These usually measure 4–6 in. (10–15cm). The two ends together usually equal one gap. Therefore, divide the finished width of 50 in. (127cm) by 9 = 5½ + ½ in. (14 + 1.3cm) left over which can be added to the edge.

Triple pleats give a very elegant outcome.

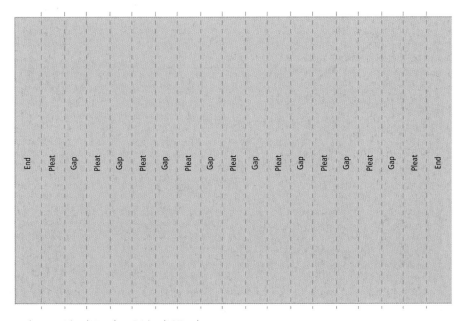

End | Pleat | Gap | Pleat | Gap | Pleat | Gap | Pleat | Gap | Pleat | Gap | Pleat | Gap | Pleat | Gap | Pleat | Gap | Pleat | End

9 pleats x 6 in. (15cm) = 54 in. (135cm)
8 gaps x 5½ in. (14cm) = 44 in. (112cm)
2 ends = 3½ + 2½ in. (8 x 7cm) = 6 in. (15cm)

Total: 104 in. (262cm)

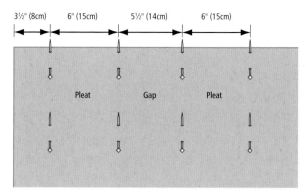

3½" (8cm)   6" (15cm)   5½" (14cm)   6" (15cm)

Pleat   Gap   Pleat

1. Press the top of the curtain on both sides, taking out the pins along the top edge. The buckram will adhere to the fabric under the heat of the iron and this will help to keep all the layers together. On a flat surface and with the front side facing, mark the pleat positions with a craft pin pointing upward right at the top of the curtain edge. It is important to be accurate so the pleats will sit vertically. At the leading (inside) edge it looks better to have more than half a gap to allow for the overlap, so the first pin mark will be at 3½ in. (8cm). Continue along the top edge of the curtain, alternating pleat and gap measurements to the outside edge. This should be 2½ in. (7cm). If it does not appear correctly, check the measuring and alter if necessary. ◄

4. Using a longer stitch on the sewing machine, stitch the pleats. Start ¼ in. (6mm) from the top, reverse back up to the top to reinforce and then stitch to the bottom of the pleat. Once again back stitch (reverse) to add strength. Leave 12 in. (30cm) of thread at the beginning and end of the stitching for finishing the pleats off. Repeat on all the pleats. ◄

5. Holding the top of the curtain with the left hand, with the left index finger in the pleat, use the right hand to push the center fold in to form the triple effect. Make sure the pleat is even before squeezing the buckram, as it can be difficult to alter once creased. Pin with a craft pin at the base of the pleat, just below the buckram. Repeat on all the pleats. A clothes peg can be used.

2. Repeat along the bottom edge of the buckram, making sure the pleats will be vertical (use a set square to check that the pleats are 90 degrees to the edge). ▼

3" (7.5cm)

3. Bring the pleat lines together, making sure the top edges are even. Take out the pin and push through the fabric. Take out the back marker and push the pin all the way through the layers. It is best to push the pin through at an angle. Do the same with the bottom pin. ▲

design NOTE
If the pleats are small, double pleats can be made instead of triple, and it will still allow the fabric to drape well.

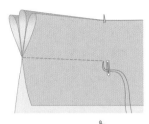

8. Press the curtains, lining side first, and then insert the pin hooks close to the pleat. Also insert hooks at the two ends.

9. Hang the curtains onto the pole or track and allow them to fall into folds. It may be necessary to run your fingers from the pleats downward to form the folds. Tie long strips of lining around the curtains to allow them to hang correctly into the folds. Leave the strips for a few days.

6. With the top side of the machine stitching facing, pull through the long threads at the bottom of the pleat. Secure the bottom of the pleat with a couple of double-thread stitches and then push the needle through to the top of the pleat. Neatly oversew with 10 stitches. (You could stitch a covered button on at this point.) Repeat on all pleats. ▼

7. Hold the top of the pleat with the left hand and with double thread, sew the top. First sew a couple of stitches to secure the machine stitching and then sew each pleat section separately. Finish off securely.

Goblet pleats

These are made in exactly the same way as the triple pleat, until the top of the pleat is stitched. It is secured at the top by making a few stitches and then the pleat is opened out to give the goblet shape. Gently push out the pleat until the desired shape is achieved. Sew a few stitches ³/₈ in. (1cm) either side of the machine stitching to hold it open and finish securely. Push batting or padding inside the goblet to achieve the shape. Insert the hooks as before.

Goblet pleats provide an ideal finish for dress curtains.

Inverted pleats

These are made in the same way as triple pleats, but a single pleat is taken through to the reverse side of the curtain, giving a smooth invert on the front. Press the pleats flat and stitch them to secure.

Very smooth, clean lines are achieved with inverted pleats.

Box pleats

With box pleats, the single pleat is on the front of the curtain. Stitch the lower edge of the pleat very neatly, just below the buckram. Where box and inverted pleats are used, the curtains do not pull back as far as triple pleats and may be best used as fixed dress curtains.

Box pleats can also be used on fixed valances.

Eyelet curtains

These curtains are becoming very fashionable and require only 1½ times the width of the window. The eyelets, which are available in several metallic finishes, are slotted easily onto a pole.

The curtains are made in the same way as for pinch pleated curtains (see pages 98–99) however, at the top, the excess folded fabric is trimmed to 1 in. (2.5cm). This is to avoid extra thickness where the eyelets are placed.

There must always be an even number of eyelets and eight per finished width. Measure from the center of the pole to the wall. The gap between the eyelets must not be more than twice this measurement as the curtain will not run smoothly—every 8–10 in. (20–25cm). Make sure an eyelet does not occur on a seam. The inside and outside edges should be approximately 4 in. (10cm).

Make sure the eyelets match the curtain pole for the most stylish look.

SKILL LEVEL
• 3

ADDED REQUIREMENTS
• Eyelets

SEE ALSO
• Valances, p96

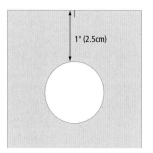

1" (2.5cm)

1. Establish the size of the hole to be cut out by making a template in cardboard. Try the process in spare fabric. The hole must not be too big, otherwise the eyelet edge will not catch the fabric securely and the fabric will pull apart.

Press the top edge to allow the buckram and fabric to adhere together and keep a row of pins underneath the buckram. Position the eyelets 1 in. (2.5cm) from the top edge.

Place the fabric onto a flat surface. On the wrong side of the curtain, place a pin at the top edge to mark the center of each eyelet. Use the template to mark the eyelet positions with a marker.

2. Cut with a pair of sharp scissors. Place the front part of the eyelet through from the front of the fabric. Using your fingers, press the fabric around the ring so the fabric snags on the hooks. Place the back of the eyelet on top and press so that it clips together. Squeeze all around the ring to secure. Repeat for each eyelet.

Lift off the pole and thread the eyelets onto the end, leaving the last one to go beyond the support. The curtains will hang naturally into folds.

Puffed heading

These curtains have an attached flounce at the top that hangs over the top of the heading, usually in a contrast fabric.

SKILL LEVEL
• 1

ADDED REQUIREMENTS
• Contrast fabric
• Narrow heading tape

SEE ALSO
• Lined curtains, p70

1. Follow the instructions for Lined curtains, steps 1–14 (see pages 70–72).

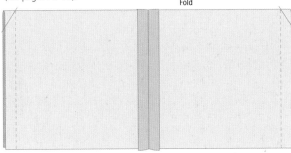

2. Decide on the finished length of the frill. Double this amount and add on 1¼ in. (3cm) seam allowance in total. Cut the same number of widths as the curtain. Join together and press the seams open, trimming to 1 in. (2.5cm). Fold in half lengthwise with right sides together and pin the side edges. The total width must match the curtain, so adjust the seam allowance accordingly. Stitch. Trim off the corners and turn through. Press, pushing out the corners.

3. Place the frill panel to the right side of the upper curtain edge. With the raw edges level, pin and sew together with ⅝ in. (1.5cm) seam allowance. Press open.

4. Pin narrow heading tape over the seam, enclosing all the raw edges. Turn under the corners of the tape and pull out the cords.

5. Stitch both edges in the same direction and across the ends.

6. Press the curtains, pull up the cords to achieve the correct measurement and insert the hooks. Hang onto the track or pole and arrange the frill if necessary.

Sheer curtains

Sheer curtains are made from lightweight, translucent fabrics, and are traditionally used to give privacy. There is such a beautiful array of color and design that they can be the only curtains at the window, giving a summery, light feel to a room. The fabrics are available in many widths so seams will not always be necessary.

SKILL LEVEL
• 1

TOOLS
• Scissors
• Soft tape measure
• Metal tape measure
• Sewing kit

MATERIALS
• Fabric
• Thread (Madeira monofil clear thread can be used)
• Net pleat tape/curtain wire

SEE ALSO
• Curtains, p62
• Fabric characteristics, p38
• Hand stitches, p42
• Machine stitches, p51
• Seams and hems, p54

Sheers can be hung on poles or on a combination track with curtains. Use a fine heading tape to give gentle folds and hang with hooks, or slot the curtains on a pole through the loops at the back of the tape.

If the sheers are to be hung as net curtains, you can make a simple casing and slot plastic curtain wire through.

Sheer curtains require 2½–3 times the width of the window to give the best effect.

1. To cut the fabric, allow 6 in. (15cm) at the hem and 4 in. (10cm) at the top. Make sure the fabric is square; the best way to do this is to pull a thread and trim to this line (see page 38). It is helpful to lay the fabric against a table corner or straight edge and weight it down so that it will not slip. Measure the length required and mark across the fabric on the grain line. Cut and mark the top right side of each piece. Although it may seem that there is little difference, it may not show until the curtains are hanging that one width is upside down or back to front.

3/8" (1cm)

2. If it is necessary to join fabric widths together, a French seam will be the most professional and neatest seam (see page 55). Cut off the selvages, as they can be tight. Pin the widths together starting at the bottom edge and working upward. Any differences in length can be adjusted at the top where they will not be seen. Machine stitch the widths together using French seams and press.

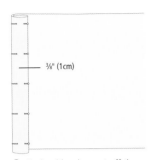

3. At the side edges cut off the selvage. Fold over ⅜ in. (1cm) twice toward the wrong side and pin. Machine close to the edge.

4. Press up 6 in. (15cm) at the hem to the wrong side and then fold in half. Machine close to the top of the hem, leaving 12 in. (30cm) thread to sew up the ends.

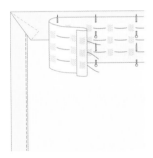
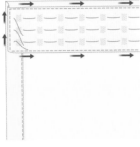

5. Lay the fabric onto a flat surface, wrong side up, mark the finished length, and fold over to the wrong side. Trim to 1½ in. (4cm). Pin net pleat tape to the curtain ⅛ in. (3mm) from the top. Tuck under the corners to conceal the raw edges. Do not sew over the cords as they will be knotted when pulled up to the correct width.

6. Stitch on the sewing machine, starting at the bottom left-hand side. Go up to the top, along the top and down the other side. Go back to the bottom left side and machine along the bottom edge. This will prevent the tape from twisting.

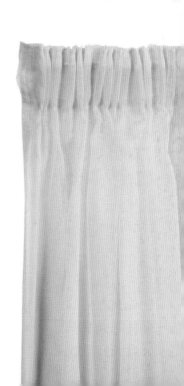

technique NOTE
If the fabric is lightweight, you can weight it at the hem by slotting in lead weight tape.

Tiebacks

Tiebacks are a useful way of holding back curtains during the day, to let the maximum amount of light into a room. They can also be a design feature. They can be made from leftover fabric or contrasting fabric, thick cord, beads, and tassels.

Curved piped tieback

This is a simple but stylish tieback that can be made from leftover fabric, and contrast piping can be used to define it. A gathered or pleated frill can be added to the bottom edge.

To establish the length required, place a tape measure around the curtains and pull them back so the outside edge is in line with the end of the curtain pole or track. The curved shape dips down in the center. Cut a template in paper or spare lining to confirm the correct shape.

SKILL LEVEL
• 2

TOOLS
• Soft tape measure
• Sewing kit
• Zipper foot

MATERIALS
• Fabric, 12 in. (30cm)
• Lining, as above
• Craft-weight interfacing
• Piping cord, 46 in. (3m) per pair
• Tieback hooks
• Brass rings

SEE ALSO
• Trimmings, p186
• Hand stitches, p42
• Machine stitches, p51

1. Cut two pieces of fabric, two of lining and two of craft-weight interfacing, allowing ⅝ in. (1.5cm) seam allowance all round. When cutting the fabric, take care to position the template to allow both tiebacks to display the fabric pattern at its best (see cutting plan below). Cut enough piping strips on the cross/bias to go round both tiebacks. They may have to be joined together, but these joins can often be hidden at the back.

Selvage

Bias strips for piping

Center line

Cutting plan: Position the front and back pieces so that the pattern design (if applicable) is correct and the center line is parallel to the selvage.

2. Place the fabric on top of the interfacing and pin together at right angles to the edge. ▼

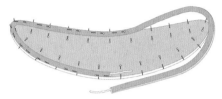

3. To make the piping, see page 187. Starting at the bottom of the back, place on the edge of the tieback, pinning close to the cord. Overlap the edges and trim overlay at ⅝ in. (1.5cm). Join the two ends together (see page 188). Cut the piping cord and butt together. Fold over the piping and pin over the join. ▼

4. Using a zipper foot on the sewing machine, stitch round the piping carefully, stitching over the right-angled pins. Remove the pins. If you require a frill, stitch it on at this stage. ▼

5. Place the lining and fabric right sides together and pin from the interfacing side, allowing the previous stitching to be seen. Follow this line of stitching or closer to the piping if possible. Stitch all around using the zipper foot, leaving a 6 in. (15cm) gap at the bottom edge. ▼

6. Trim the interfacing to ⅛ in. (3mm) and graduate the seam allowances, particularly around the corners (see note on page 55).

7. Turn right side out by separating the lining from the fabric and interfacing, and feeding through the gap at the bottom edge. Be careful not to split the stitching at the sides. ▼

Lining

8. On the lining side, pin along the top edge. Now pin the opening together, turning in all the raw edges. Slip stitch. Take out all the pins and press. ▼

9. Stitch brass rings on to the ends using a double thread and placing stitches evenly around the ring. Place the tieback round the curtain to establish the hook position, which should allow the curtains to hang straight down at the outside edge.

Braided tiebacks

These are three tubes filled with batting, braided together. They are usually made from self-colored fabric or a mixture of self-colored and contrasting fabrics.

SKILL LEVEL
• 2

ADDED REQUIREMENTS
• Batting
• ⅜ in. (1cm) wide strong tape

SEE ALSO
• Curved piped tieback, p92

1. Cut 6 strips of fabric 6 in. (15cm) wide by 1½ times the required length (one width of fabric, selvage to selvage can be used) and 6 strips of medium-weight polyester batting.

2. Cut a length of flat tape 60 in. (1.5m). Place the tape on top of one layer of fabric and one of batting. Stitch along the top edge securely. Fold in half lengthwise and machine stitch down the side edges, allowing ⅝ in. (1.5cm) seam allowance, enclosing but not catching the tape. Use a longer stitch because of the thickness of the fabrics.

3. You may need to have help at this point or tie the tape round a door handle. At the stitched end, pull apart the fabric to allow the tape to be pulled through. Make sure that the fabric stays apart and carefully pull the tape. This gradually threads the tube through to the right side.

The fabric should be braided tightly for a professional-looking finish.

4. Cut off the tape and repeat until all the tubes are made. With all the seams at the center back of the tubes, place three together, overlapping the edges. Pin together allowing ⅝ in. (1.5cm) seam allowance. This is machined across, so it may be necessary to pull out and trim off some of the excess batting. Braid together tightly and pin together at the other end.

5. Confirm that the tieback length is correct by placing it around the curtain. Shorten if necessary. Machine stitch across the end and remove any excess batting. ▼

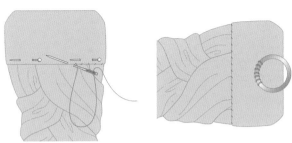

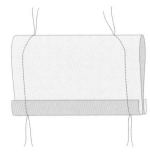

7. Graduate the seam allowance and turn through to the front. Press and then place onto the tieback ends, pushing the tieback in as far as possible. Pin the front and back securely. Slip stitch all around the tieback. Place a brass ring onto the back of the end cap, allowing ⅝ in. (1.5cm) to be seen. Stitch securely and place around the curtain to establish the hook position.

6. To make end caps, cut 4 x 4 in. (10cm) square pieces of fabric. Fold in half right sides together, fold over ⅝ in. (1.5cm) (to the wrong side) and pin the sides with ⅝ in. (1.5cm) seam allowance. At the fold increase the seam allowance to ¾ in. (2cm) to give a curved shape.

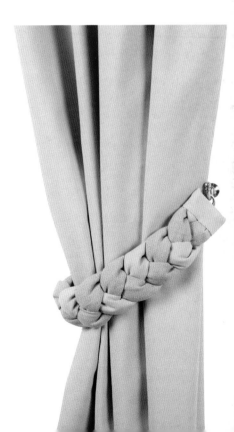

The hook should be positioned to allow the curtains to hang straight down at the outside edge.

Valances

Valances are made from lengths of fabric one-sixth of the length of the curtains, and are placed either on a valance track as part of a combination with the curtains or on a pelmet of wood along with café curtains, net or voile curtains, or a shade. They can be placed high above the window frame to create an illusion of greater length, will cover the curtain track, and give a stylish finish.

Valances are usually made from the same fabric as the curtains. An extravagant heading can be used on the valance, which may take more widths of fabric, covering curtains with less fullness.

If the fabric has a pattern repeat, this must be taken into consideration, both when calculating the quantity required and also the most appropriate design. Curved shapes can be created by using paper patterns.

Lined valance with pencil pleat heading

If the curtains are lined, the valance should also be lined. Pencil pleat heading will require 2½–3 times the width.

1. Cut fabric widths, adding 4 in. (10cm) to the length (for patterned fabric, cut the full pattern repeat, see Fabric characteristics, page 38). Cut lining widths to the exact finished length.

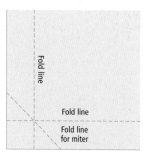

Fold line

Fold line

Fold line
for miter

2. Join the widths, matching the pattern and taking 1 in. (2.5cm) seam allowance on the lining. Press the seams open and snip the selvage every few inches. Press 2 in. (5cm) along the bottom and side edges to the wrong side.

3. At the corners, make a 45-degree miter (see page 59). Open out the folded edges and fold the corner point inward until the creases are on top of each other. Fold the side and bottom edges inward to finish the miter. Press.

SKILL LEVEL
• 1

TOOLS
• Scissors
• Metal tape measure
• Soft tape measure
• Sewing kit

MATERIALS
• Fabric
• Lining
• Thread
• Heading tape
• Track or pelmet board
• Curtain hooks or touch-and-close fastener

SEE ALSO
• Curtains, p62
• Fabric characteristics, p38
• Hand stitches, p42
• Machine stitches, p51
• Seams and hems, p54

technique NOTE
If a pelmet board is used, a special pencil pleat tape can be obtained that will attach to the hook side of a touch-and-close fastener.

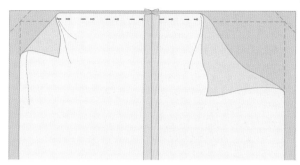

4. To attach the lining, open out the hem edge. Match up the center of the fabric and the lining at the bottom edge, right sides together. Pin toward the sides, taking care not to stretch the fabric or lining, stopping 2 in. (5cm) from the miter. Stitch on the sewing machine using ⅜ in. (1cm) seam allowance. ➤

5. Press the lining upward, enclosing the hem. At the sides, trim off any excess lining (more than ⅜ in. [1cm] wider than the fabric), and fold under the lining to reveal ⅜ in. (1cm) fabric. Pin into place.

6. Using the outer-colored thread, stitch up the miter with a ladder stitch (see page 45). With lining-colored thread, stitch the side and bottom corners up to the machine stitching. ▼

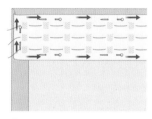

8. Stitch on the sewing machine close to the edge of the tape, from the bottom left side, up to the top, along the top, and down the other side. Return to the left side and stitch along the bottom edge. This prevents the tape from twisting. ▼

Exact finished length

7. Place the valance, lining side up, onto a flat surface and measure the required finished length. Fold over and pin. Place the heading tape ⅛ in. (3mm) from the top edge and pin through all thicknesses. At the sides, tuck the tape 1 in. (2.5cm) under the corner of the folded fabric and pin. Pull out the cords as these will not be stitched.

9. Remove all the pins, press, and pull up the cords to the required width. If there are several widths it is a good idea to pull the cords from both ends. Adjust, making the gathering even, and insert the curtain hooks.

Lined valance with pinch pleat or goblet pleat heading

Pinch pleat and goblet pleat headings will require double the width of the curtains.

SKILL LEVEL
• 2

ADDED REQUIREMENTS
• Buckram
• Pin hooks
• Craft pins

SEE ALSO
• Lined valance, p96
• Other headings, p82

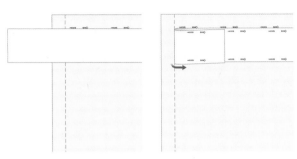

1. Follow steps 1–5 for the Lined valance (see pages 96–97). Place the valance wrong side up onto a flat surface. Mark the required finished length with a line of pins (on the wrong side of the fabric). Place the top edge of the buckram on this line, overlapping the side edges by 5 in. (12.5cm). Pin the buckram to the fabric along the top and bottom edges using the craft pins, taking care to keep the fabric smooth. At the side edges, fold over the buckram on the crease line of the side edge to give a double layer.

2. Baste along the top edge (see page 44). The bottom edge is stitched with a herringbone stitch (see page 47).

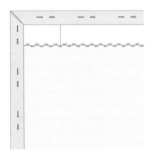

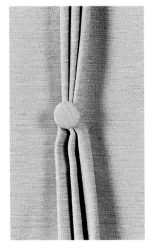

Add a decorative button for extra style.

3. Fold the top edge over the buckram and transfer the pins from the buckram, through all the layers. Miter the corners as in step 3 on page 96, and ladder stitch to close (see page 45). Take out the pins from the bottom edge of the buckram.

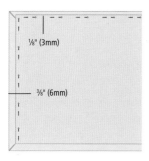

⅛" (3mm)

⅜" (6mm)

4. Smooth the lining up to the top and tuck underneath, leaving ⅛ in. (3mm) of fabric showing. Pin the sides of the lining, trimming it if necessary, as in step 6 on page 97.

5. Slip stitch all the edges. Press, lining side first and then the right side. The buckram will adhere, which is helpful when making the pleats.

3" (9.5cm)

6. To calculate the pleat positions, see pages 84–85. Pin the pleats together and stitch, removing all the pins and leaving 12 in. (30cm) of thread at both ends of the pleat. This is used to complete the pleating process (see pages 85–86).

Goblet pleat

7. Press the valance and insert the pin hooks close to each pleat. To complete the goblets, see page 87.

Pinch pleat

Pin hooks are inserted so that the valance can be hung on a valance track.

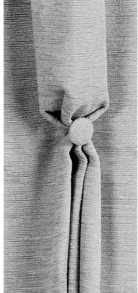

Lined valance with contrast or frilled trim

Add a designer's touch with a contrast trim, fringing, or frill at the bottom edge.

SKILL LEVEL
• 1

ADDED REQUIREMENTS
• Fabric for contrast

SEE ALSO
• Lined valance, p96

1. Follow steps 1 and 2 for Lined valance, page 96.

2. To prepare the contrast trim, for a 1 in. (2.5cm) length, double this measurement and add 1¼ in. (3cm) seam allowance, so 3¼ in. (8cm) strips are required. Cut across the fabric from selvage to selvage and join together using 1 in. (2.5cm) seam allowance. ➤

3. Fold in half lengthwise, right sides together (at one end only), and stitch the end, using ⅝ in. (1.5cm) seam allowance. Trim off the corner close to the stitching and turn through to the right side. Carefully push out the corner. Fold in half, right sides out, and press the length of the trim.

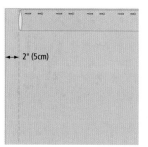

2" (5cm)

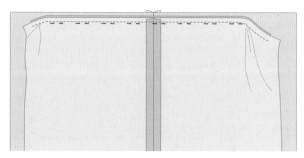

4. Pin the trim to the bottom edge of the valance right sides together, starting 2 in. (5cm) in from the selvage and taking ⅝ in. (1.5cm) seam allowance. At the other end, cut the trim 1⅜ in. (3.5cm) in from the selvage. Place right sides together and machine the edge, taking ⅝ in. (1.5cm) seam allowance. Trim off the corner and turn through to the right side. Press with your fingers and pin into place. ▼

5. Stitch using the sewing machine on the pin line.

6. Pin the lining to the main fabric at the bottom edge, right sides together, working on the lining side where the stitching line of the trim is visible. Start from the center and work outward. ▼

7. At the side edges, pin the main fabric to the back around the trim, and join to the lining. Trim to ⅝ in. (1.5cm) and press toward the center.

Trim off corner

8. Stitch on the sewing machine just below the previous stitching line. Trim off the corners and graduate the seam allowances, leaving the fabric longest.

9. Turn through to the right side, press the lining side first and then the right side, so the fabric sits smoothly above the trim and no stitches show through.

10. Continue, following steps 7–9 on page 97.

11. The gathered frill will usually be 2⅜–3 in. (6–7.5cm) deep. Double this and add 1¼ in. (3cm) seam allowance. Therefore, 6½–7¼ in. (15–18.5cm) strips are required. Twice the number of strips will be needed to gather correctly. Follow step 3, stitching both ends of the frill. Gather the frill (see page 53) in sections and pull up to the correct width.

2" (5cm)   2" (5cm)

12. Pin the frill to the bottom edge of the valance, right sides together, starting in the center and working outward. Match up the joins and pull up the gathering to fit. Start and finish 2 in. (5cm) in from each edge. Machine stitch just below the gathering stitches. Continue as above and complete as for the lined valance.

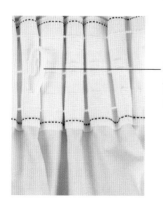

The hook positioning allows full coverage of the track.

Shades

As with curtains, the style of the shade you choose will determine the fabric quantities and type required, but in general, shades require less fabric as they fit tighter to the window.

What works where

Shades are simple window treatments that make a bold statement in a room. They take a relatively small amount of fabric, so can provide an opportunity to splash out on an expensive fabric design. They equally look smart when a plain fabric is used to combine with a neutral décor.

Shades can be placed inside the recess (perhaps hung along with curtains) or outside the recess, covering all the edges of the window and blocking out all the light. This method also hides any discrepancies in the walls (tiles or an architrave can alter the straight edge of a wall).

Shades can be hung on a simple wooden batten with the use of a touch-and-close fastener, a ratchet system, or a sidewinder system (see pages 28–29).

When choosing a patterned fabric, take care when positioning the shade so that the pattern is centralized to achieve the maximum effect.

Use the natural light afforded by even small windows to maximize the properties of the fabric and its overall design.

design NOTE
For shade design possibilities, see the Design directory, pages 210–213.

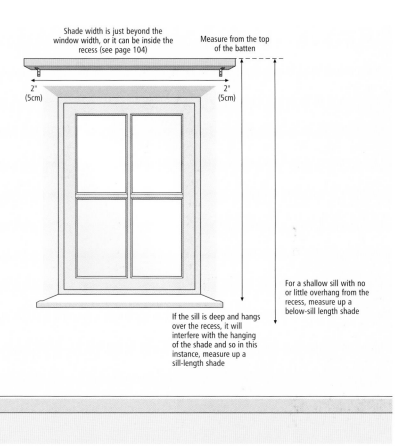

Shade width is just beyond the window width, or it can be inside the recess (see page 104)

Measure from the top of the batten

2"
(5cm)

2"
(5cm)

For a shallow sill with no or little overhang from the recess, measure up a below-sill length shade

If the sill is deep and hangs over the recess, it will interfere with the hanging of the shade and so in this instance, measure up a sill-length shade

Checklist for shades

Copy this checklist, fill it in, and take it with you to the fabric store.

FABRIC

Design _____
Color _____

LINING

Lined ☐
Unlined ☐
Interlined ☐

STYLE

Roman ☐
Cascade ☐
Roll-up ☐
Austrian ☐

MEASUREMENTS

Width _____
Length _____

ACCESSORIES

Track and batten ☐
Pull cord ☐
Chain control ☐
Trim ☐

Calculating fabric

You need just enough fabric to cover the window. Add 3 in. (8cm) to the width and 6 in. (15cm) to the length. When more than one width is required, the pattern repeat must be taken into consideration (see page 39). One full width will be in the center and part widths will be stitched to the sides. It may be possible to turn the fabric onto its side to eliminate the need for joins, but this can only happen when the required length is less than the width of the fabric (less a minimum of 4 in. [10cm] for hems) and the pattern can be turned.

For the lining, add 1½ in. (4cm) to the finished width of the shade. The length has to accommodate the rod pockets. These pockets will contain the rods that give the shade its structure. Each pocket is 2 in. (5cm) and they should appear at 8–12 in. (20–30cm) intervals, depending on the length of the shade (the shorter the shade, the closer the pockets). Therefore, add 2 in. (5cm) for each pocket required plus 6 in. (15cm) for the hems.

The batten can be placed inside the recess

When the shade is to hang inside the recess, make sure the width is the same at the top and bottom, and that the length is the same down each side. The shade should be ¼–½ in. (0.5–1cm) narrower than the recess opening.

A roll-up shade gives an informal look that is well suited to kitchens and bathrooms.

Austrian shade
You will need twice the width of the window and 12 in. (30cm) added to the length, for both the fabric and the lining. The pattern repeat must be taken into consideration on the fabric and extra must also be allowed for a frill.

Roll-up shade
Add 1½ in. (3cm) to the finished width and 12 in. (30cm) to the length, for both the fabric and the lining.

To work out the position of the rod pockets

1. If the finished length of the Roman shade is 56½ in. (141cm) and requires four pleats, subtract 2½ in. (6cm) (2 in. [5cm] for the top to allow for the fixing and ½ in. [1cm] extra for the bottom pleat) = 54 in. (135cm).
Divide this by the number of pleats (rod pockets) required:
54 in. (135cm) ÷ 4½ (or nine half pleats; there is always a half pleat at the bottom).
54 in. (135cm) ÷ 9 = 6 in. (15cm). This is a half pleat, therefore a whole pleat = 12 in. (30cm).

2. Turn under and press 1 in. (2.5cm) on each side of the lining (toward the wrong side). Fold the lining in half lengthwise to check that the bottom edge is perfectly square and adjust if necessary. Then place the fabric on a table, so that one corner of the fabric lies over one corner of the table, ensuring that the fabric is at 90 degrees.

1"
(2.5cm)

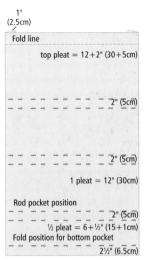

Fold line

top pleat = 12+2" (30+5cm)

2" (5cm)

2" (5cm)

1 pleat = 12" (30cm)

Rod pocket position

2" (5cm)

½ pleat = 6+½" (15+1cm)

Fold position for bottom pocket

2½" (6.5cm)

3. On the front side of the lining, mark the rod pocket positions (with a horizontal pin), working up from the bottom edge. The first mark to be made is the fold position for the bottom pocket 2½ in. (6.5cm) up from the edge. Continue upward, marking the pocket positions.

4. Mark across the fabric at each side, in the center, and also in between (every 10–12 in. [25–30cm]), depending on the width of the shade. This will enable accurate positioning. (The rod pockets must be at right angles to the edge and perfectly horizontal to allow the shade to pull up evenly.) Fold the lining in half widthwise, to confirm that the pocket positions are correct. Adjust if necessary.

Pocket = 1"
(2.5cm)

5. Fold the pockets together, remove the pins at the back and pin together, as if you were making large tucks. Recheck the pin line to confirm the exact pocket measurement (1 in. [2.5cm]) and adjust if necessary. If the pockets are uneven, the rods will not pull up correctly.

6. Stitch on the sewing machine, stitching one end and along the width. Secure the thread ends and leave 12 in. (30cm) for finishing off later.

7. Proceed to position the lining onto the fabric, following the instructions on pages 107–109.

Roman shades

Roman shades produce a clean, lined, uncluttered look. They can be pulled high up to allow as much light in as possible. They are not complicated to make, but do require accurate measuring and the ability to use a sewing machine.

Roman shades are economical and a small quantity of an expensive fabric can add a touch of glamor to a simple furnishing scheme.

Unlined, sheer fabrics can be used as an alternative to net curtains, and cottons, cotton mixes, silks, and slightly heavier fabrics are all suitable. Large patterns are not practical as the design will be lost when the shade is folded up. However, a dramatic stripe, check, or geometric design can be very effective.

Roman shades will enhance the appearance of windows where curtains would be impractical.

SKILL LEVEL
• 1

TOOLS
• Scissors
• Metal tape measure
• Soft tape measure
• Sewing kit
• Junior hacksaw
• Staple gun

MATERIALS
• Fabric
• Lining
• Thread
• Plastic or brass rings
• Plastic or wooden rods
• Plastic, aluminum, or wooden bottom bar
• Cord
• Screw eyes
• Cleat hook
• Fixing mechanism: wooden batten and touch-and-close fastener, corded headrail, or sidewinder mechanism

SEE ALSO
• Shades, p102
• Fabric characteristics, p38
• Hand stitches, p42
• Machine stitches, p51
• Seams and hems, p54
• Suspension systems, p24

Lined Roman shade

Most fabrics will give a much more professional finish if they
are lined, and this also protects the fabric from strong sunlight.
Blackout lining can be used in a bedroom and interlining can be
sewn in to produce a sumptuous and cozy finish.

1. Measure the window (see pages 102–103). To cut the fabric,
add 3 in. (8cm) to the width and 6 in. (15cm) to the length.
When joining two widths of fabric together, make allowance for
the pattern repeat (see page 39). One full width will be in the
center and part widths on the sides. Centralize the pattern so
that the main design appears in the center of the shade. Mark
with pins or a chalk line and measure outward to the required
width. Mark once again and confirm that this line is parallel to
the selvage. Do not include the selvage in your measurements
as it should not be used and make sure the fabric is straight/
square (see page 38). Measure the required length and cut.

2. To cut the lining, add 1½ in.
(4cm) to the width and 2 in.
(5cm) for each rod pocket to
the length. The pockets are
evenly spaced and 8–12 in.
(20–30cm) apart.

3. Pin, then press 1½ in. (4cm)
in on each side of the fabric and
1 in. (2.5cm) in on the lining.
Check that the width is correct.
At this stage you can alter the
turning width to achieve the exact
measurement.

4. Calculate the positions of the
rod pockets on the lining (see
page 105).

6. Pin the lining onto the fabric.
Place the fabric wrong side up on
the table. Position the lining right
side up onto the fabric, making
sure the gap on either side is
even, and the bottom edges are
together. Pin the lining and fabric
together just underneath the
bottom rod pocket, making sure
that the pocket is horizontal and
the measurement to the bottom
edge is correct. Adjust if necessary.

7. Smooth the fabric and pin
the next pocket once again,
confirming the measurement is
exact. Continue all the way up the
shade, pinning the pockets and
sides. Stitch the sides with lining-
colored thread using a slip stitch.
Where the rod pockets appear,
reinforce the stitching.

5. Pin and sew the rod pockets
using a sewing machine. Fold
along each pocket with wrong
sides together. Stitch 1 in. (2.5cm)
from the fold to create the pocket.

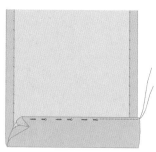

8. To make the bottom pocket, press up 2½ in. (6.5cm) at the bottom edge. Fold under ⅝ in. (1.5cm) and pin. Tuck under the corners and machine stitch close to the edge, leaving 12 in. (30cm) of thread. This thread is used to stitch the side edges when the bottom bar has been inserted.

9. Measure the exact finished length. Fold over the top edge and pin. Trim to ⅝ in. (1.5cm). Measure the exact finished width of the touch-and-close fastener and pin onto the top edge of the shade (⅛ in. [3mm] from the top). Tuck in the corners of the fabric under the tape to conceal all the raw edges. Machine stitch from the bottom left-hand corner, up to the top, along the top, and down the other side. Return to the starting point and machine stitch along the bottom edge. This method prevents the tape from twisting.

10. Mark the position of the rings 2¾ in. (7cm) in from each edge and then divide evenly between them (no more than 20 in. [50cm] apart). Use a double thread to sew on the rings securely to the bottom edge of the rod pocket, trying just to sew the front edge, so that the rod is not hindered.

11. At the same position use the main fabric thread color to stitch through to the front to secure the fabric and lining. Use double thread, lift up the pocket, and make a few stitches on top of each other (see Stab stitch, page 49).

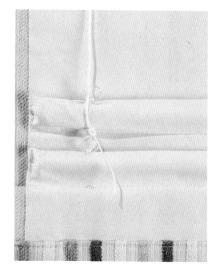

The cord pulling through the rings provides a Roman shade with its signature fold-up mechanism.

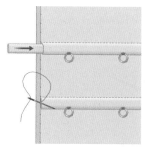

12. Cut plastic or wooden rods ¾ in. (2cm) shorter than the pocket. Cut the bottom bar 1¼ in. (3cm) shorter than the finished width. Insert carefully and stitch the ends with the reserved thread.

13. Press the shade and place (lining side up) onto a flat surface. Cut a length of cord for each line of rings. Each length will vary as it runs up the shade, across the tops and down the other side (allow 39 in. [100cm] on this side). Securely knot one end to the bottom ring. Thread upward through the rings to the top, along the tops and down the side. Repeat for all lengths of the cord.
➤

14. Attach touch-and-close tape to a wooden batten and use a staple gun to secure firmly. Insert screw eyes to the underneath of the batten in corresponding positions to the rings.

15. To hang the shade, attach to the wooden batten joining the touch-and-close fastening tape securely. Lift up the shade and feed the cords through the screw eyes. Allow it to drop down and check that it is hanging correctly. Adjust the touch-and-close fastener if necessary. Pull the shade up and down to test and when it is at maximum length, the cords can be knotted together just beyond the last screw eye. Braid them together to prevent tangling. To secure the shade, wind the cord around a cleat hook fixed to the wall.

Interlined Roman shades

Sewing a layer of interlining between the fabric and lining produces a sumptuous finish, but will require slightly different techniques and more hand sewing. When using thick fabric, the interlining should be trimmed at the fold line to avoid bulkiness below the touch-and-close fastener.

SKILL LEVEL
• 3

ADDED REQUIREMENTS
• Interlining

SEE ALSO
• Lined Roman shade, p107
• Hand stitches, p42
• Seams and hems, p54

design NOTE
Shades lined with blackout lining are made in the same way as lined shades, but are heavy and may have pinholes that show light through where the fabric has been pierced with stitches. They are useful in bedrooms to prevent light shining through a single layer of fabric of a Roman shade. They are often used to accompany sheer or voile curtains.

1. Follow steps 1–4 of Lined Roman shade (see page 107).

2. Cut the interlining to the same size as the fabric. On a flat surface, place the fabric wrong side up. Lay the interlining onto the fabric, matching the centers and pinning along the center line from top to bottom (vertically). Interlock the interlining (see Lock stitch, page 46), using fabric-colored thread. The tiny stitches should not show, but it is best to use outer fabric color, just in case. Continue to interlock in vertical lines toward the edges, pinning and stitching 12 in. (30cm) apart.

3. Open out the side edges and fold the interlining along the creased edge. Interlock along the edge. When using a thick fabric, cut the interlining along this edge, as it becomes too thick if it is folded. For lighter-weight fabrics, the interlining is folded along with the fabric and then secured when the side edges are stitched.

4. Press up 2½ in. (6.5cm) at the bottom edge. Miter the corners (see page 59). Sew along the side and bottom edges using herringbone stitch (see page 47). Use ladder stitch to sew up one corner at the hem (see page 45). The other corner is left open to insert the bottom bar.

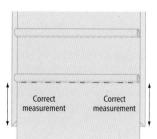

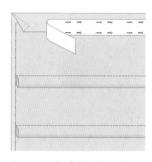

5. Pin the lining onto the fabric. Place the fabric wrong side up on the table. Position the lining right side up onto the fabric, with an even gap on either side and the bottom edge of the lining overlapping the shade by 2½ in. (6.5cm). Pin the lining and fabric together underneath the bottom rod pocket. ▼

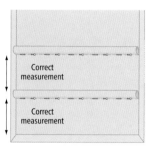

6. Smooth the fabric and pin the next pocket again. Continue all the way up, pinning the pockets. At the bottom edge, trim the lining to 1 in. (2.5cm) above the bottom edge. Fold under 1 in. (2.5cm) and pin. ▼

7. Stitch the sides and bottom edge with lining-colored thread using a slip stitch (see page 42). Reinforce the stitching at the rod pocket positions.

8. Lay the fabric lining side upward, and measure the finished length. Fold over and pin. Trim to ⅝ in. (1.5cm). Measure the width of the fastener and pin onto the top edge of the shade. Tuck in the corners of the fabric under tape to conceal raw edges. Machine stitch from the bottom left-hand corner, up to the top, along the top, and down the other side. Return to the starting point and machine along the bottom edge, to prevent the tape from twisting.

9. To complete the interlined shade, follow steps 10–15 for the Roman shade (see pages 108–109). On step 12, insert the bottom bar and miter the corner using ladder stitch.

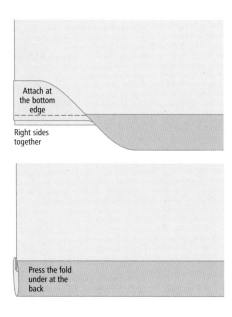

Attach at
the bottom
edge

Right sides
together

Press the fold
under at the
back

Cascade shades

These shades are very similar to Roman
shades. The gap between the rod pockets
decreases as you move up the shade, so
more of the pleats are visible, giving a
cascading effect. The rod pocket calculations
differ from Roman shades but construction
is the same. ➤

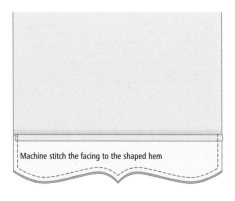

Machine stitch the facing to the shaped hem

Roman shades with contrast trims or borders

It is possible to add a border to the sides
of the shade or a contrasting fabric to the
bottom edge. These can be used to extend
the width of the shade or as a design detail
to add another color of the same fabric or a
complementary fabric that will enhance a
color scheme or unify the room design.

It is important that the fabrics are of the
same weight so they will sit together and
hang correctly. The fabric should be cut out
and stitched to the main fabric before
construction. ◀

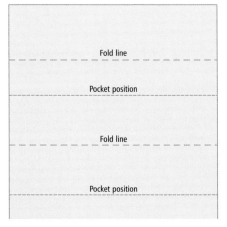

Fold line

Pocket position

Fold line

Pocket position

Roman shades with shaped hems

Shaped hems can be created simply by
adding extra length to the fabric. Cut out
the design in paper and hold it up to the
window to see how it looks before cutting
into the fabric. This can then be used as a
template for the design. Fabric selection is
important and often inspires the design.

These shades are suitable when they are
hung outside the window recess, so light
cannot come through at the bottom edge. ◀

Secure to batten with
touch-and-close
fastener

Roll-up shades

These are simple, soft shades that combine two fabrics of the same weight that are stitched together and then rolled up with the use of cords and screw eyes. The fabric is cut longer than the window and rolled up round a piece of doweling. They are softer than roller shades and can be hung at any height up the window. They are an economical way to add a touch of color.

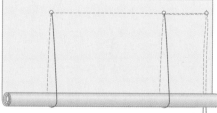

Pulling the cords rolls,
or lifts, the shade

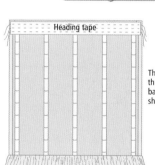

Heading tape

The cords are fed
through the horizontal
bars on the Austrian
shade tape

Attach the frill to
the bottom edge

Austrian shades

These are very different from what has been described so far. They are flouncy and frilly, and use up a much larger quantity of fabric. They can be made up in sheer fabric or printed cottons and taffetas, which, if lined, will produce a much better finish. Machine sew tapes on the reverse side at equal intervals and gather them together at the top with the use of pencil pleat tape. Feed the cords through the loops on the tape and pull them up to form the flounces.

Pull the
cords to lift
the shade

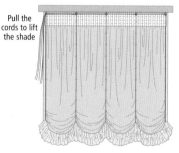

Reverse

Pelmets

These are usually made from stiff buckram or self-adhesive pelmet stiffener, and are fixed to a pelmet board above the window.

Padded straight-edged pelmet

Interlining or batting is used to give a padded appearance, and fringing or braid can be attached for decoration.

SKILL LEVEL
• 3

TOOLS
• Scissors
• Soft tape measure
• Metal tape measure
• Sewing kit
• Sharp blade
• Clothes pegs
• Staple gun or tacks

MATERIALS
• Pelmet board
• Fabric
• Interlining
• Lining
• Buckram
• Touch-and-close fastener

1. Cut the fabric, with 2 in. (5cm) allowance all around. If more than one width needs to be used, do not make a center join. Allow one full width in the center and part widths stitched onto the side edges. If you are using a patterned fabric, position the design to give the best effect.

2. Cut the interlining in the same way. Cut the lining, with 1 in. (2.5cm) allowance.

3. Cut the buckram to the exact finished measurement. With a sharp blade, score along the fold lines to allow the buckram to bend easily at the sides.

4. Place the interlining onto a flat surface. Position the buckram onto the interlining, leaving an even edge all round.

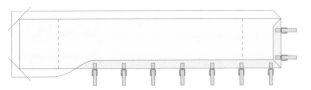

5. Dampen the edges of the buckram and fold over the interlining. Use clothes pegs to secure. At the corners trim the interlining and miter together. Allow the buckram to dry completely.

6. Place the fabric on a flat surface wrong side up. Position the buckram onto the fabric and fold over the fabric edges, mitering the corners. Pin in place. Stitch the miters.

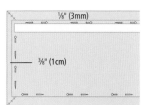

7. Pin the soft part of the touch-and-close fastener to the top edge of the lining, ¾ in. (2cm) from the top. Machine all around, taking care not to twist the tape. Fold under the edges of the lining and pin to the pelmet, allowing ⅜ in. (1cm) of fabric to be seen. At the top edge allow ⅛ in. (3mm). Slip stitch all round, using the lining-colored thread.

8. Attach the hook part of the fastener to the pelmet board. It may be necessary to use a staple gun to ensure that it sticks securely. Crease the corners and place onto the pelmet board.

The touch-and-close fastener gives a smooth, flat finish to the pelmet and makes it easy to fit the pelmet to the board.

measurements NOTE
When calculating measurements, make sure you allow a couple of inches (a few centimeters) either side of and above the curtain track. Also allow enough depth of pelmet board to pull the curtains freely.

design NOTE
Fringing or braid can be sewn or stuck on with fabric glue, before hanging onto the board.

Pillows

This chapter takes a look at one of the most popular home décor projects. Even functional pillows offer an ideal design opportunity to add complementary, accent, or contrasting colors. The possibilities for shape and decorative detail are endless, so pillows are a great way to unleash your home styling creativity.

Pillows

Pillows introduce color, pattern, texture, comfort, and style to your home, office, or garden. They are used for decorative purposes, to introduce colors to plain furniture, to blend colors together, or to give a new look to a room.

There are many different shapes of pillow—square, round, rectangular, heart, bolster, Oxford, triangular, to name but a few.

Small quantities of expensive fabric can bring a touch of glamor or splash of color to a plain room. Leftover fabric from curtains or complementary colors blend the décor of rooms together. Appropriate fabrics must be chosen—select washable fabrics for pillows that will be in frequent use.

A fantastic array of decorative trimmings is available—beads, ropes, tassels, piping cords, and contrast colors of similar fabrics.

Padding

There are many types of pillow form. Feather, synthetic fiberfill, kapok, and solid foam (usually for box pillows) are all available and in many sizes. Feather forms give the best appearance and will not lose their shape, but they are not always practical as the feathers can cause allergic reactions. However, an extra cover can be made to enclose the feather form to stop the feathers from coming through.

Fasteners

Zippers are the most common fastener, but they take a little time to sew in. A dressmaking zipper is the correct weight for a scatter pillow. When making a box pillow, a heavier zipper can be used. Always choose a matching color or one that is slightly darker than the fabric as it will be less obvious than a lighter one. Buttons are a very popular closure and can be a striking feature on the front of a pillow, when contrast or decorative buttons are used. Touch-and-close tape can be sewn on or ties can be made.

Pillow forms are available in many shapes and sizes with a variety of fillings.

Cutting

When cutting the fabric, only add ⅝ in. (1.5cm) in total for the seam allowance, as pillows always look better when they are full and plump. Wherever possible, use the selvage as a straight edge and measure a parallel line from it (but do not include it in the measurement). Follow the grain across the fabric and use a set square to mark the top and bottom edges. When a patterned fabric is being used, centralize the pattern where possible.

If you use a large pattern, mark the center point of the pattern and measure outward for the required width and length (using the selvage to confirm that the line is parallel and square). The front and back of the pillow do not have to be the same. A complementary plain fabric or contrast can be used to give two options.

measurements NOTE
The fabric measurements given in the Materials section at the beginning of each project in this section are approximate and will ultimately depend on the size of the pillow form you are using.

See pages 120–123 for cutting plans for the pillows pictured right and featured in this section.

Cutting plans

The following plans show the pieces you will need to cut from your fabric to make the projects featured in this chapter. The pieces should be marked onto the fabric using pins or a marker pen, and you should always pay attention to the pattern repeat where applicable.

Square pillow with zipper fastener

Use this cutting plan to make the pillow featured on pages 124–125.

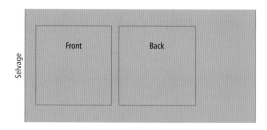

Square pillow with piped edge and zipper fastener

Use this cutting plan to make the pillow featured on pages 126–128.

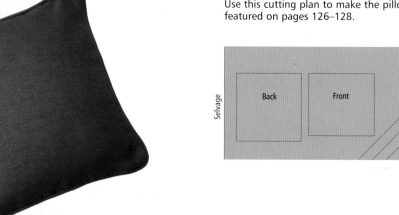

Box cushion with piping and zipper

Use this cutting plan to make the pillow featured on pages 129–131.

Front gusset

Selvage

Front	Back	Bias strips for piping

Back gusset

Oxford-style pillow

Use this cutting plan to make the pillow featured on pages 132–133.

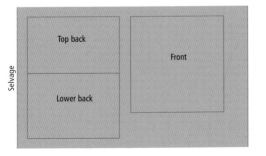

Selvage

Top back	Front
Lower back	

measurements NOTE
Exact measurements for the pieces need to be based on the size of your pillow form, so make sure you measure it accurately before cutting.

Rectangular panel pillow

Use this cutting plan to make the pillow featured on pages 134–135.

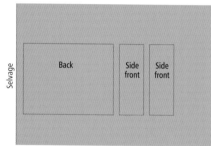

Round pillow with optional frill

Use this cutting plan to make the pillow featured on pages 136–137.

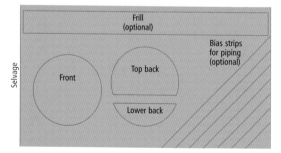

Bolster pillow with piped ends

Use this cutting plan to make the pillow
featured on pages 138–139.

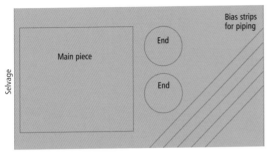

Bolster with gathered end and button detail

Use this cutting plan to make the pillow
featured on pages 140–141.

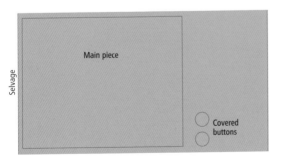

Square pillow

This is the simplest pillow design of all, and so makes a good first project. It can be made from a variety of fabrics to add a splash of color to your sofa.

SKILL LEVEL
• 1

TOOLS
• Scissors
• Soft tape measure
• Sewing kit
• Zipper foot

MATERIALS
• Fabric, 20 in. (50cm)
• Pillow form
• Thread
• Zipper, 2–4 in. (5–10cm) shorter than pillow width
• Sewing kit

SEE ALSO
• Machine stitches, p51
• Seams and hems, p54

1. To cut the fabric, measure the pillow form and add ⅝ in. (1.5cm) at the sides and ¾ in. (2cm) seam allowance to the length. Place the fabric right side upward onto a flat surface (using the corner of a table is a good idea), so the selvage lies at the side and the bottom edge is at 90 degrees.

Do not include the selvage in the measurement as this is often a tighter weave and will distort easily. It can be cut off if necessary. Measure the required width, centralizing the pattern (if applicable), and mark with a line of pins or marker pen. Use a set square to mark the bottom edge, confirming the straight grain of the fabric. Measure up and mark the top edge. Repeat for the back piece. ◄

2. Cut carefully and mark the top front side of each piece with a pin or marker pen. This is important if there is little noticeable difference between the face and the back of the fabric. ▼

3. Using a sewing machine, zigzag the bottom edge of both front and back pieces (see page 52). Place right sides together and pin the bottom edge, leaving a gap for the zipper. Stitch, reinforcing the ends.

Match striped fabric at the top to give continuity to the design.

4. Turn to the right side and press the seam allowance open. Position the zipper underneath and pin through all layers. Using the sewing machine and zipper foot, stitch all the way round the zipper ¼ in. (6mm) from the zipper center. ▼

5. Open the zipper. With right sides together, pin the other three sides together, matching the corners first. Stitch using the sewing machine with ⅝ in. (1.5cm) seam allowance. Stitch over the corners again to add strength. ➤

6. Trim the corners and then zigzag the edges together to neaten. Trim any threads and turn right side out, gently pushing out the corners. ➤

7. Press then insert the pillow form, taking care not to split the stitches at the end of the zipper. This can be done by folding the pillow form and pushing it through the opening. When inside, unfold the form and push it into the corners. Close the zipper and plump up.

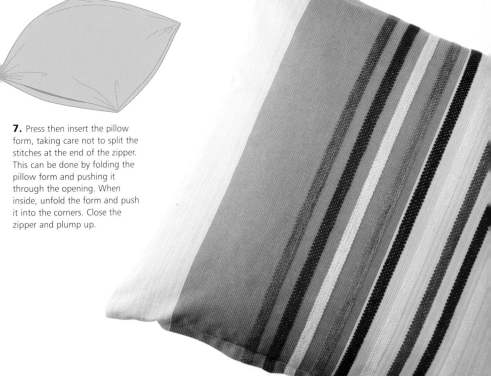

Square pillow with a piped edge

The piped edge, particularly in a contrast color, is a design
feature that makes this style of pillow stand out.

ADDED REQUIREMENTS
• Piping cord, 80 in.
  (200cm)
• Fabric for piping
• Zipper, 2–4 in. (5–10cm)
  shorter than pillow width

SEE ALSO
• Square pillow, p124
• Trimmings, p186
• Machine stitches, p51
• Seams and hems, p54

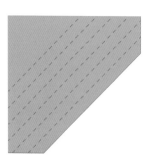

Joining the bias strips

*A concealed zipper can be
used to hide all the stitching.*

1. Follow the instructions for the
square pillow with a zipper
fastener (see pages 124–125) for
cutting out the front and back
pieces (adding ¾ in. [2cm] to the
length of the back piece, to make
it easier to sew in the zipper). For
the piping, the fabric is cut out
on the cross or bias. This is at
45 degrees and will allow the
piping to bend round the corners,
as it will stretch. The strips are
1⅜ in. (3.5cm) wide.

3. The pre-shrunk piping cord
(no. 3 cord is a good size to
use as it is not too bulky when
covered and is relatively easy to
sew in), is placed into the center
of the bias strips and pinned
together. If there are any joins,
press the seams open before
inserting the piping cord.

2. Approximately 80 in. (200cm)
of piping cord is needed for a
16–18 in. (40–45cm) pillow (you
can purchase plain flanged piping
or twisted cord). Several pieces
can be joined together to provide
enough length.

4. Starting at the bottom center
of the front piece of fabric, pin
the piping to the fabric, matching
the edges together (using the pins
from the piping). Gently bend the
piping around the corners. It is
important not to stretch the
piping as it will return to its
original size and pucker the edges.

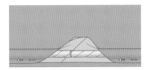

5. At the bottom edge, overlap the piping strips and cut, allowing ½ in. (1.3cm) overlap. Cut along the grain of the fabric. Cut the piping cord so that it butts together (see top picture, above). Place the piping strips right sides together and pin at ¼ in. (7.5mm) seam allowance (see bottom picture, above). Stitch and press the seam open with your fingers.

6. Pin across the piping to complete and, using the zipper foot on the sewing machine, stitch all around the pillow close to the piping cord.

7. Zigzag the bottom edge of the front and back pieces. Place the open zipper, right sides together onto the bottom edge of the front piece. Pin through all the layers on the piping stitching line.

8. Stitch close to the zipper teeth, using the zipper foot. When reaching the head of the zipper, insert the needle into the fabric, lift up the presser foot, slide the zipper head along and replace the presser foot. Continue to the end of the zipper. Do not stitch right to the end of the zipper tape.

9. Place the bottom edges right sides together, pin, allowing an extra ¼ in. (6mm) on the back piece. This extra fabric will make the stitching of the zipper easier. Pin from the front side from the zipper ends out toward the corners. Pin through the stitching line of the piping. Stitch using the zipper foot, taking care not to catch the zipper ends.

The zipper is at the bottom of the back of the pillow and so is concealed.

10. Turn to the right side and place flat on a surface. Evenly pin the seam allowance under. Close the zipper and transfer the pins through all the layers. Stitch using the zipper foot on the right side, taking care not to catch the fabric and zipper from the opposite side. ◀

11. Open the zipper and, with right sides together, pin the other three sides, matching up the corners first. Pin on the piping stitching line, or inside this line, to make the piping as tight as possible. Stitch using the zipper foot. ▼

12. Trim round the corners and any piping joins. Zigzag the edges together to neaten.

13. Turn right side out and press. Carefully fold the pillow form and insert it into the pillow, taking care not to split the ends of the zipper. Push the form into the corners, close the zipper and plump up the pillow.

Beaded trimming, fringing, or flanged cord can be used instead of piping in these instructions (see pages 190–191).

Box cushion

Box cushions have a gusset and usually contain a solid foam filling. They are used on garden furniture, benches, or window seats. They can be square, rectangular, round, or shaped to fit a specific space.

It is important to use durable fabrics such as cotton, linen union, and damask. If a bold pattern is used, the pattern on the gusset should match the top and the base.

A zippered opening allows the cover to be cleaned easily. The zipper is stitched into the gusset strip and goes around to the sides a few inches to ease the insertion of the foam pad. Piping made from the same or a contrast fabric can be inserted into the seams.

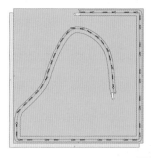

SKILL LEVEL
• 2

TOOLS
• Scissors
• Soft tape measure
• Sewing kit
• Zipper foot

MATERIALS
• Fabric, 40 in. (1m) per cushion, depending on size of foam filling
• Foam pad
• Thread
• Zipper, 8 in. (20cm) longer than cushion width
• Fabric for piping
• Batting (if necessary)

SEE ALSO
• Fabric characteristics, p38
• Trimmings, p186
• Machine stitches, p51
• Seams and hems, p54

1. To cut the fabric, measure the foam and add ⅝ in. (1.5cm) all around. Cut the top and base of the cushion, taking care to centralize the pattern and follow the grain (see page 38). ▼

2. For the gusset, measure the depth and add 1¼ in. (3cm). Measure all around the foam for the length. The zipper section will be placed along one edge and up to 3 in. (7.5cm) into the adjacent sides (depending on the zipper length). Subtract this from the total and add 2 in. (5cm) for tolerance. Add 1¼ in. (3cm) to the depth of the gusset where the zipper is to be placed and cut lengthwise to produce two halves. The zipper will be inserted here. Cut the piping strips on the bias (see page 186), stitch together the required amount, and pin the piping cord into the center.

3. Mark the center of all sides of the top and base with a small snip into the fabric or a fabric marker pen. Starting at the center back of the top and with right sides together, match the edges and pin the piping in place around the edge. Take care not to stretch the piping. Place the fabric on a flat surface and lay the piping on top. Take out the pin from the piping and secure it through all the layers. It is only necessary to remove every other pin from the piping. At the corners the piping edge can be snipped to ease the placement. It looks better to round the corner as it will fit snugly around the foam. Take care to repeat the same shape at each corner.

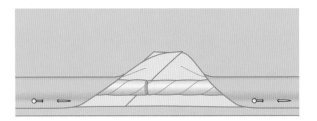

4. Overlap the piping strips and trim one side, allowing a ½ in. (1.3cm) overlap. Cut along the grain. Cut the piping cord so that it butts together.

5. Place the strips right sides together and pin, taking ¼ in. (6mm) seam allowance. Stitch and press open with your fingers.

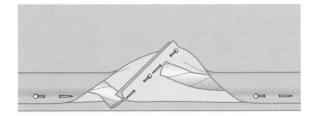

6. Pin across the piping to enclose and lay the fabric on the foam to check that the piping sits on the edge of the foam perfectly. Adjust if necessary. Stitch all around using the zipper foot on the sewing machine. Repeat on the base.

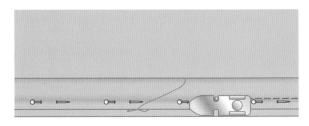

The zipper extends around to the side to allow easy insertion of the cushion pad.

7. Prepare the gusset for the zipper. Zigzag stitch the two edges that will join to the zipper (see page 52). Mark the center of both pieces. Pin these edges under to the wrong side ⅝ in. (1.5cm). Pin the bottom edge close to the teeth and place the top edge over the teeth to conceal the zipper. Pin ⅜ in. (1cm) from the edge, making sure that the center marks match up.

The piping gives crisp edges to the cushion.

8. Machine stitch both sides of the zipper on the pin line, removing the pins as you stitch, using the zipper foot. This can be basted first if you prefer. With right sides together and matching the center marks on the back of the top and the zippered gusset, pin together from the top side. This enables you to follow the stitching line of the piping. ➤

9. At the corners it may be necessary to snip the gusset (within the seam allowance) to pin the layers together. When the gussets meet, pin together, taking ⅜ in. (1 cm) seam allowance. Stitch and trim any excess fabric. Zigzag together and pin away from the zipper. Open the zipper. ➤

10. Pin the bottom edge to the gusset, matching up all the markings and snipping the seam allowance where necessary. ➤

11. Stitch using the zipper foot on the previous piping stitching line. It is a good idea to stitch around again to strengthen the stitching. It is easier to stitch close to the piping cord if the pins have not been removed. ▽

12. Trim the corners and zigzag the edges together. Trim any loose threads. Turn right side out and press. Insert the foam pad, taking care not to break the stitches at the sides of the zipper. Push the seam allowances toward the gusset, allowing the piping to sit upright on the right side.

● ● ● ● ● ● ● ● ● ●

technique NOTE
If the cushion pad seems loose, a thin layer of batting can be stitched around the foam.

SKILL LEVEL
• 1

TOOLS
• Scissors
• Soft tape measure
• Sewing kit
• Zipper foot

MATERIALS
• Fabric, 30 in. (75cm)
• Pillow form
• Thread
• Zipper, 2–4 in. (5–10cm)
  shorter than pillow
  width, or touch-and-close
  fastener

SEE ALSO
• Machine stitches, p51
• Seams and hems, p54

Oxford-style pillow

This pillow is easily made and the flange edging is achieved by top stitching.

This pillow has a 1½–2 in. (4–5cm) attached border all around. Take this into consideration when deciding on the size of the pillow form, as it can appear very large if an 18 in. (45cm) form is used. You will need to decide on the border width before you start.

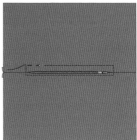

1. To cut the front, add twice the border width plus ⅝ in. (1.5cm) to the size of the pillow form. To cut the back, the width is the same as the front. The back length is dependent on the fastener used. For a zippered back, add 1¼ in. (3cm) to the length. For the touch-and-close fastener, add 1¾ in. (4cm) to the length. Mark the top right side of all the pieces.

2. For the zippered back, cut the back in half across the width. Zigzag the center edges (see page 52). With right sides together, pin the two center edges together, leaving a gap for the zipper.

3. Stitch, taking ⅝ in. (1.5cm) seam allowance. Turn to the front and pin back the seam allowance. Place the closed zipper underneath the gap and pin, transferring the pins from the fabric through to the zipper. Pin and sew the lower edge close to the zipper teeth and the upper edge ⅜ in. (1cm) away. This will overlap the teeth and be less visible. Open the zipper.

4. With right sides together, pin the edges with a ⅝ in. (1.5cm) seam allowance. Machine stitch. Trim the corners and press the seams open as far as possible into the corners. This will make it easier to achieve crisp edges. Turn through to the right side and press the edges.

5. Mark the stitching line for the border accurately with pins or a marker pen. Stitch using the sewing machine on the marked line. It is a good idea to stitch around again on the same line to add strength. For an added design detail, a satin stitch can be used, possibly in a contrast color.

6. Insert the pillow form and spread into the corners. Plump up.

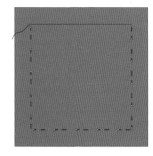

Touch-and-close fastener

1. Follow step 1 for cutting out.

2. Fold over the edges ⅜ in. (1cm) and machine stitch the fastener onto both edges. The fastener stops ⅜ in. (1cm) from the edge of the fabric, as it is very stiff. Press together and continue to make as left, following steps 4–5.

The touch-and-close fastener is a simple and effective way of temporarily enclosing the pillow form.

Rectangular panel pillow

This stylish pillow is made from a combination of two fabrics. A plain fabric is used for the sides and back, and a touch of class can be added in the center by using a small quantity of an expensive fabric.

SKILL LEVEL
• 2

TOOLS
• Scissors
• Soft tape measure
• Sewing kit
• Zipper foot

MATERIALS
• Fabric, 20 in. (50cm) for each panel
• Pillow form
• Zipper, 2–4 in. (5–10cm) shorter than pillow width

SEE ALSO
• Square pillow, p124
• Machine stitches, p51
• Trimmings, p186
• Seams and hems, p54

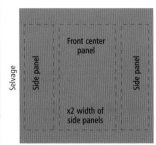

1. Select your fabrics and decide on the proportion for the pillow front. The center panel is usually twice the width of the side panels. The back of the pillow is plain and looks good if the same fabric is used on the side panels. If a patterned fabric is used for the center panel, centralize the main feature of the pattern (if applicable) with care.

Cut the pieces carefully, making sure the fabric is square (follow the instructions for the Square pillow on page 124), adding ⅝ in. (1.5cm) seam allowance to the sides and ¾ in. (2cm) at the lower edge, to make sewing in the zipper easier.

2. Stitch the front and side panels together, taking ⅝ in. (1.5cm) seam allowance (see page 52). Zigzag stitch the edges separately and press the seams open. If the center panel is a lighter-colored fabric, zigzag the seams together and press toward the outer edge. If you are using a lighter-weight fabric for the center panel, it is a good idea to select a piece of curtain lining or similar type of fabric to back the front section.

3. Before stitching the front and side panels together, you can insert a beaded edge or piped edge (see pages 186–191).

The smooth piped edge adds interest when using plain colored fabrics.

5. Zigzag the bottom edges of the front and back. An invisible zipper can be used, but inserting it requires an invisible zipper foot and a higher skill level. If you are using an ordinary zipper, follow steps 3–4 of making a square pillow (see pages 124–125). Undo the zipper.

6. With right sides together, join the other three sides together matching the corners first and pin, taking ⅝ in. (1.5cm) seam allowance. Stitch, pivoting at the corners. Double stitch the corners. Trim the corners and zigzag both edges together. Trim any threads, turn through and press, gently pushing out the corners.

4. If you choose a piped edge, it is unnecessary to use bias strips or piping cord. Stitch the piped edge to the center front section, matching the edges together and using ⅝ in. (1.5cm) seam allowance. Stitch the sides to the center front enclosing the piping. Zigzag the edges together and press away from the trimming. ▼

7. Fold the pillow form and insert it into the pillow, taking care not to split the ends of the zipper opening. Push into the corners and close the zipper. Plump up.

Round pillow

This pillow can be made from any type of fabric, and complementary piping or a frill will define its circular shape.

SKILL LEVEL
• 1

TOOLS
• Scissors
• Soft tape measure
• Sewing kit
• Zipper foot

MATERIALS
• Fabric, 20 in. (50cm)
• Pillow form
• Thread
• Zipper, 2–4 in. (5–10cm) shorter than pillow diameter

SEE ALSO
• Machine stitches, p51
• Seams and hems, p54
• Gathering and frills, p180

1. To cut the fabric, measure the diameter of the pillow form and add ⅝ in. (1.5cm). Take a piece of paper to make a pattern and fold into four. Mark the cutting line with a pencil and string or with a tape measure, carefully rotating from the point. Mark the fold points.

2. Cut the back pattern piece two-thirds of the way down to accommodate the zipper. Place onto the fabric, adding ⅝ in. (1.5cm) seam allowance to the cut edges. Take care to position any pattern centrally and that the grain of the fabric is followed. Mark the quarter sections on the outside edge.

3. With right sides together, pin the back pieces together, taking ⅝ in. (1.5cm) seam allowance and stitch the ends, leaving a gap for the zipper (see page 52). Zigzag the edges. Turn to the right side and fold under the seam allowance. Pin the seam allowance. Place the zipper underneath and pin the lower edge close to the zipper teeth. Position the top edge over the zipper teeth and pin at ⅜ in. (1cm). Stitch all round the zipper using the zipper foot. Open the zipper.

The width of the frill should be proportionate to the size of the pillow.

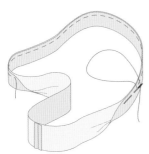

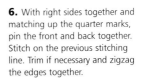

6. With right sides together and matching up the quarter marks, pin the front and back together. Stitch on the previous stitching line. Trim if necessary and zigzag the edges together.

7. Turn right side out, press, and insert the pillow form.

4. Double the circumference measurement and cut strips of fabric 5 in. (12.5cm) wide for a 2 in. (5cm) finished frill. Join the widths together, press the seams open, and fold in half lengthwise.

5. Gather into four sections. Pull up the threads and pin onto the front pillow, matching the four marker points. Make sure the gathers are even, and stitch.

The zipper is concealed in the seam at the back of the pillow.

Bolster pillows

Bolster pillows are cylindrical in shape and are often used on beds or at both ends of sofas.

The plain piped ends reveal more of the fabric pattern.

Bolster with piped ends

This pillow looks very stylish when the piping is made from a contrasting color of fabric.

1. To cut the fabric, measure tightly around the circumference of the pillow form and add 1¼ in. (3cm) seam allowance. Measure the length and add 1¼ in. (3cm). To make a pattern for the end, fold a piece of paper 2 in. (5cm) larger than the diameter of the pillow form into quarters. With a piece of string or pair of compasses, draw a line measuring the radius plus ⅝ in. (1.5cm).

2. Cut through all four layers, mark the fold points, open out, and place onto the straight grain of the fabric (see page 38). Cut and mark the four quarters with a small snip or marker.

3. With right sides together and using the main piece of fabric, pin the long edges together, taking ⅝ in. (1.5cm) seam allowance and leaving a gap for the zipper. Stitch and press the seam open. Zigzag the edges (see page 52). Turn through to the right side and pin under the seam allowance. Place the zipper underneath and pin one side close to the teeth and the other side at ⅜ in. (1cm), covering the teeth. Using the zipper foot, stitch all around on the line of the pins, removing them as you go. If you prefer, this can be basted first. Open the zipper.

4. Prepare the piping strips and pin the piping into the center of the strip (see pages 187–188). With right sides together, pin the piping to the circle, taking care not to stretch the piping. ▼

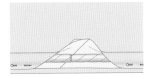

5. Remove a pin from the piping and push it through all the layers. Overlap the ends by ½ in. (1.3cm). Cut one edge, following the grain of the fabric. Cut the piping cord to butt together. ➤

6. Place the piping strips right sides together and stitch, taking ¼ in. (6mm) seam allowance. Press the seam open and enclose the piping cord. ➤

7. Stitch all around the circle using the zipper foot. Repeat for the other circle. ▲

8. Divide the main fabric tube into four sections. Mark with a snip or marker. ▼

9. With the zipper open and right sides together, pin the circles to the ends of the fabric, matching up all the quarter markings. It may be necessary to snip the main fabric when pinning to the circles. Stitch using the zipper foot (from the circle side to follow the previous stitching line). Stitch the other end.

10. Zigzag the seams together and trim if necessary. ▼

11. Turn right side out, press and insert the pillow form, taking care not to split the ends of the zipper.

Bolster with a gathered end and button detail

For this bolster, it is a good idea to use a lightweight fabric such as cotton or chintz, as thicker fabrics will not gather easily.

SKILL LEVEL
• 2

ADDED REQUIREMENTS
• Two buttons

SEE ALSO
• Hand stitches, p42

1. To cut the fabric, measure the length of the pillow form plus the diameter of the end. Add 1¼ in. (3cm). Measure around the circumference of the pillow and add 1¼ in. (3cm).

2. With right sides together, pin the long edges together, taking ⅝ in. (1.5cm) seam allowance. Stitch the seam. Zigzag the edges and press the seam open.

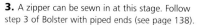

3. A zipper can be sewn in at this stage. Follow step 3 of Bolster with piped ends (see page 138).

The large covered button hides the rows of gathering stitches.

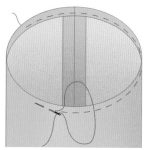

4. Turn right side out. Press under ⅝ in. (1.5cm) at each end. With a double thread, hand sew a row of gathering close to the folded edge (see page 48).

5. Insert the bolster form and position equally.

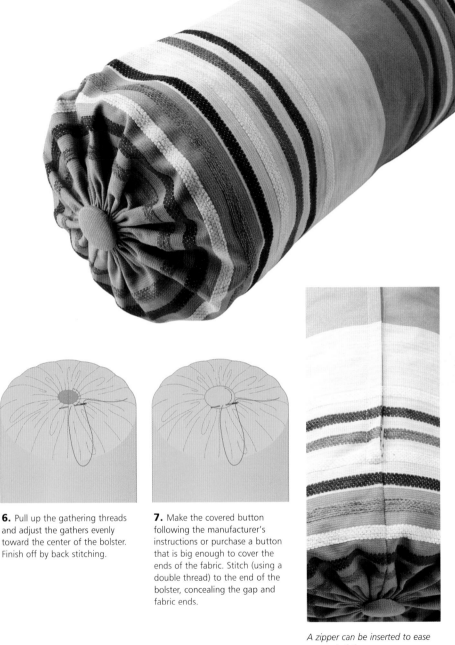

6. Pull up the gathering threads and adjust the gathers evenly toward the center of the bolster. Finish off by back stitching.

7. Make the covered button following the manufacturer's instructions or purchase a button that is big enough to cover the ends of the fabric. Stitch (using a double thread) to the end of the bolster, concealing the gap and fabric ends.

A zipper can be inserted to ease removal of the cover.

Bed and table linen

The focal point of a bedroom will be the largest item, which is probably the bed. It should be dressed in a style that gives you the atmosphere you want and that will suit the room. Similarly, the table can be the focal point of a kitchen or dining room, and can be covered not only to protect it but also to make it a more stunning interior feature. This chapter gives the instructions for making all the essential elements—duvet covers, sheets, pillowcases, bed skirts, tablecloths, placemats, and napkins—and offers the opportunity of adding your own design touches along the way.

Bed linen

Crisp cotton and cotton polyester mixes are ideal for creating a sleek look, especially when used on duvet covers. For a more feminine look, frills, piping, and pleats can be added. Popper tape, buttons, or ties can be used as closures.

What works where

The clean lines given by a duvet with a popper-tape closing mechanism, a fitted sheet, an Oxford-style pillowcase, and a bed skirt with box pleats are well suited to a contemporary interior. A duvet with ties, a pillowcase with a frill edging, and a gathered bed skirt add more detail and interest—livening up an otherwise plain décor or perhaps suiting a traditional country look. Decorative elements can be added to pillowcases to add interest or they can be made in contrast fabrics to unify the color scheme, combining with curtains or Roman shades.

On the more practical side, you should consider the style and size of bed and mattress—for example, if the bed has a base this will need to be covered with a bed skirt; if the mattress is particularly heavy you may prefer a fitted sheet over a flat sheet for easier changing of the bedding when it requires washing. Even if the bed does not have a base, you could add a bed skirt to create concealed storage.

Calculating fabric

Standard bedding sizes vary between countries—and sometimes even within a country—so it is always advisable to work from the measurements of the bedding you are looking to furnish. You will also need to take into account any frills, edgings, ties, or other decorative details you may wish to add.

Duvet covers

Duvet covers come in the following standard sizes:

U.S. NAME	U.S. SIZES
Twin	67 x 87 in. (170 x 220cm)
Full	76 x 87 in. (193 x 220cm)
Queen	87 x 90 in. (220 x 230cm)
King	104 x 92 in. (264 x 234cm)
California/Western King	110 x 96 in. (280 x 244cm)

U.K. NAME	U.K. SIZES
Single	53 x 79 in. (135 x 200cm)
Double	79 x 79 in. (200 x 200cm)
King	91 x 87 in. (230 x 220cm)
Super King	102 x 87 in. (260 x 220cm)

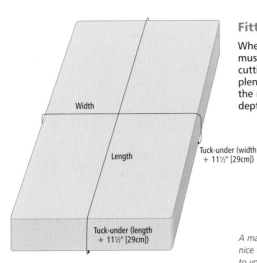

Width

Length

Tuck-under (width
+ 11½" [29cm])

Tuck-under (length
+ 11½" [29cm])

Fitted sheets

When making fitted sheets, the mattress must be measured to provide accurate cutting instructions. Generally, to allow plenty of tuck-under, add 11½ in. (29cm) to the mattress width and length plus twice the depth (including the seam allowance).

A matching covered headboard is a nice touch and can be added easily to your bedroom ensemble.

Pillowcases

Standard pillows measure 30 x 20 in. (75 x 50cm), but it's advisable to measure the specific pillows you wish to cover.

Bed skirts

Each bed base must be measured to provide accurate cutting measurements, bearing in mind the skirt should touch the floor for a professional look, and the choice of gathered frill or box pleat trim will affect the amount of fabric required. Add ½ in. (1.5cm) all around the base for the top piece, which will not be seen. Add 3 in. (7.5cm) to the skirt length for the hem allowance. See page 162 for details on fabric calculation for the alternative skirt designs.

Duvet covers

Duvet covers are made from sheeting fabric or something of similar weight that can be easily laundered. Different colors or patterned fabrics can be used to make the cover reversible and match the rest of the bed linen. They are made with a popper tape fastening, buttons and buttonholes, or ties and can be trimmed with lace or frills.

SKILL LEVEL
• 1

TOOLS
• Scissors
• Soft tape measure
• Sewing kit
• Zipper foot

MATERIALS
• Sheeting fabric
• Thread
• Popper tape

SEE ALSO
• Bed linen, p144
• Fabric characteristics, p38
• Machine stitches, p51
• Seams and hems, p54

measurements NOTE
Please refer to page 144 for a guide to bedding sizes and fabric measurements for this section.

Twin/Single duvet cover with popper tape fastening

This is the simplest duvet cover to construct and the closure is made using purchased popper tape.

1. Cut two pieces of fabric (see page 144 for duvet cover measurements), adding 1¼ in. (3cm) to the width and 2⅝ in. (6.5cm) to the length, taking care to cut the fabric along the straight grain (see Fabric characteristics, page 38). ▼

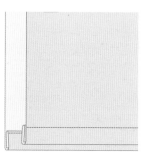

2. Make a double 1 in. (2.5cm) fold along the bottom edge of both pieces toward the wrong side. Pin and machine stitch close to the hem edge. Mark the center of each piece with a pin or marker pen.

3. Cut a length of popper tape measuring 40 in. (100cm). (For a double or king size cover, you will need 55 in. [140cm].) Separate the two strips of tape and mark the center of each piece. Pin to the folded edges of the cover, matching the center marks and working outward toward the outside edges.

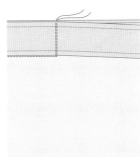

6. Finish off the duvet cover with a French seam to add strength and to neaten the raw edges (see page 55). With wrong sides facing, pin the other three edges together, taking ¼ in. (6mm) seam allowance. Stitch and trim the corners. Turn inside out and pin with right sides together, taking ⅜ in. (1cm) seam allowance. Machine stitch. Turn right side out and press.

4. Stitch close to the edge of the tape using the zipper foot on the sewing machine, taking care not to stretch the tape. Confirm that the two sides will match together before you sew the second side.

5. Press the studs together and pin the two outside edges alongside the hem line. Stitch from the outside edge to just beyond the end of the tape, and pivot to stitch at a right angle, enclosing the raw edges. Stitch again to reinforce as this area will be under strain when the poppers are pulled apart.

Poppers provide an easy open and close mechanism.

technique NOTE
A serger or overlocker (see page 13) can be used to neaten the edges of the cover. In this case, pin the pieces together with right sides facing and machine, taking ⅝ in. (1.5cm) seam allowance. Serge the edges, turn through, and press, carefully pushing out the corners.

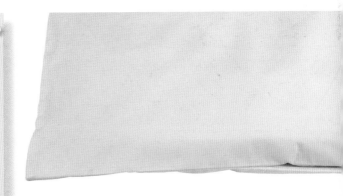

Full/Double duvet cover with buttons and buttonholes

This duvet cover is simple to make and the button and buttonhole fastening produces a neat finish.

SKILL LEVEL
• 1

TOOLS
• Scissors
• Soft tape measure
• Sewing kit
• Buttonhole foot

MATERIALS
• Sheeting fabric
• Thread
• Buttons

SEE ALSO
• Bed linen, p144
• Fabric characteristics, p38
• Machine stitches, p51
• Seams and hems, p54

1. Cut two pieces of fabric (see page 144 for duvet cover measurements), adding 1¼ in. (3cm) to the width and 2⅝ in. (6.5cm) to the length, taking care to cut the fabric along the straight grain (see Fabric characteristics, page 38). ▼

2. Make a double 1 in. (2.5cm) fold along the bottom edge toward the wrong side. Pin and machine stitch close to the hem edge. Mark the center of each piece with a pin or marker pen.

3. Mark the positions for the buttons and buttonholes 10 in. (25cm) apart, starting in the center and working outward. Five buttons will be sufficient for a double or king size duvet cover. Make the buttonholes on the sewing machine and sew on the buttons in the corresponding positions.

A buttoned opening is suitable for lightweight fabrics as it allows for a soft edge.

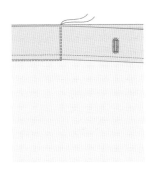

5. Use a French seam to finish off the duvet cover to add strength and to neaten the raw edges (see page 55). With wrong sides facing, pin the other three edges together, taking ¼ in. (5mm) seam allowance. Stitch and trim the corners close to the stitching. Turn inside out and pin with right sides together, taking ⅜ in. (1cm) seam allowance. Machine stitch. Turn right side out and press.

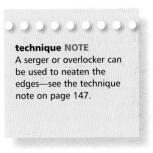

technique NOTE
A serger or overlocker can be used to neaten the edges—see the technique note on page 147.

4. The buttons remain inside the cover and are not decorative, so flat, plain buttons are best. Insert the buttons into the buttonholes and pin the outside edges right sides together alongside the hem line. Machine stitch along this line and pivot to stitch at a right angle toward the edge. Stitch again to reinforce.

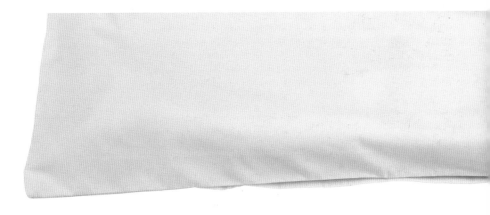

King duvet cover with ties

This duvet cover is a little trickier to make, but looks attractive and can have contrast ties to add detail.

SKILL LEVEL
• 1

TOOLS
• Scissors
• Soft tape measure
• Sewing kit

MATERIALS
• Sheeting fabric
• Thread

SEE ALSO
• Bed linen, p144
• Fabric characteristics, p38
• Seams and hems, p54
• Hand stitches, p42
• Machine stitches, p51

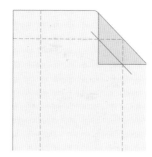

2. To make the ties, press the fabric in half, lengthwise. Open out and then press ½ in. (13mm) all around. Miter the corners by folding the corner inward to the inner crease point (see page 59).

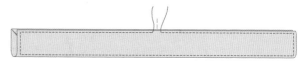

3. Fold the fabric together again, pin, baste if desired, and machine all around close to the edge. Start stitching in the center of the long side, as this is where it will be cut in half and the stitching line will not be broken where it could be visible.

1. Cut two pieces of fabric (see page 144 for duvet cover measurements), adding 1¼ in. (3cm) to the width and length, taking care to cut the fabric along the straight grain (see page 38). Cut two facing pieces the same width by 3 in. (7.5cm) and five ties 3 x 24 in. (7.5 x 60cm). These will be cut in half once prepared. ◤

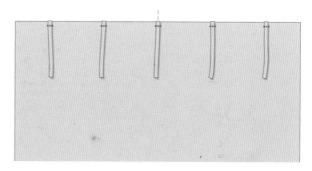

4. With right sides facing, position the ties on the lower edges of the cover evenly, 12 in. (30cm) apart, starting at the center point. Machine across each tie twice for added strength, taking ½ in. (13mm) seam allowance.

5. On one long edge of each facing, make a double ¼ in. (6mm) fold. Pin and stitch close to the edge. With right sides together, pin the unfinished edge of the facings to the lower edge of the cover, taking ⅝ in. (1.5cm) seam allowance so that the stitching on the ties is hidden. Stitch.

6. Finish off the cover with a French seam to add strength and neaten the raw edges (see page 55). With wrong sides facing, pin the other three edges together, taking ¼ in. (5mm) seam allowance. Stitch and trim the corners close to the stitching. Turn inside out and pin with right sides together, taking ⅜ in. (1cm) seam allowance. Machine stitch.

7. With the facing pressed out flat and right sides together, pin the outer edges together close to the facing seam line for 12 in. (30cm). Stitch from the outside edge on this line and pivot to stitch at a right angle toward the facing hem edge.

8. Fold the facings toward one side and secure at the sides with a few stitches to stop the facing from moving and to give a slight envelope effect to keep the quilt inside the cover.

Ties add decorative detail to an otherwise plain cover.

technique NOTE
A serger or overlocker can be used to neaten the edges—see the technique note on page 147.

Duvet cover with a false sheet flap and popper tape

This cover can be made of self-fabric or with a contrast fabric (of similar quality and weight) that forms the lower front section and gives the appearance of a sheet folded over the top edge. It can be decorated with ribbons applied across the width of the cover, lace on the edge, embroidery or appliqué, or pin tucks or small pleats can be formed on the top section.

SKILL LEVEL
• 1

TOOLS
• Scissors
• Soft tape measure
• Sewing kit
• Zipper foot

MATERIALS
• Sheeting fabric
• Thread
• Optional ribbons, embroidery floss, or lace
• Popper tape

SEE ALSO
• Bed linen, p144
• Fabric characteristics, p38
• Tucks and pin tucks, p182
• Machine stitches, p51
• Seams and hems, p54

1. Cut the back piece of fabric (see page 144 for duvet cover measurements), adding 1¼ in. (3cm) to the width and 2⅝ in. (6.5cm) to the length, and cutting the fabric along the straight grain (see page 38). The front piece is cut in two sections. The top piece will give the best appearance if it is 16 in. (40cm) in length. Add 4 in. (10cm) for the fold and 1¼ in. (3cm) seam allowance and 1¼ in. (3cm) to the width. Pin tucks or pleats require extra fabric and this amount must also be added to the length (see page 182). For the lower section, add 2⅝ in. (6.5cm) to the length and 1¼ in. (3cm) to the width.

2. With right sides together, join the upper to the lower front sections, taking ⅝ in. (1.5cm) seam allowance. Pin and machine stitch. Zigzag the edges to neaten (see page 52). Press to form the pleat. Pin across the cover, making sure that the pin line is directly over the previous stitching line. Machine across this line, basting first if preferred.

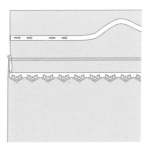

3. A second stitching line ¼ in. (6mm) above adds strength and looks attractive. At this stage, ribbon can be stitched across the width, lace attached to the lower edge of the pleat, and pin tucks or pleats can be made.

4. Make a double 1 in. (2.5cm) fold along the bottom edge of both pieces toward the wrong side. Pin and stitch close to the hem edge. Mark the center of each piece with a pin or marker.

5. Cut a length of popper tape measuring 40 in. (100cm). (For a double or king size cover, you will need 55 in. [140cm].) Separate the two strips of tape and mark the center of each piece. Pin to the folded edges of the cover, matching the center marks and working outward toward the outside edges.

6. Stitch close to the edge of the tape using the zipper foot on the sewing machine, taking care not to stretch the tape. Confirm that the two sides will match together before you sew the second side.

7. Press the studs together and pin the two outside edges alongside the hem line. Stitch from the outside edge to just beyond the end of the tape and pivot to stitch at a right angle, enclosing the raw edges. Stitch again to reinforce as this area is under strain when the poppers are pulled apart.

8. Finish off the duvet cover with a French seam to add strength and to neaten the raw edges (see page 55). With wrong sides facing, pin the other three edges together, taking ¼ in. (5mm) seam allowance. Stitch and trim the corners. Turn inside out and pin with right sides together, taking ⅜ in. (1cm) seam allowance. Machine stitch. Turn right side out and press.

Ribbons and tucks accentuate the flap detail.

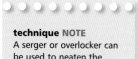

technique NOTE
A serger or overlocker can be used to neaten the edges—see the technique note on page 147.

Fitted sheets

Fitted sheets make bed-making very easy and provide a smooth finish to the mattress. They can be made to fit any depth of mattress and are usually made from sheeting fabric or a purchased flat sheet. Elastic is threaded through slots to produce a snug fit.

SKILL LEVEL
• 1

TOOLS
• Scissors
• Soft tape measure
• Sewing kit
• Safety pin
• Metal rule or set square
• Tailor's chalk or marker pen

MATERIALS
• Sheeting fabric
• Thread
• Elastic

SEE ALSO
• Machine stitches, p51
• Seams and hems, p54

1. Cut one piece of fabric, adding 10¼ in. (26cm) plus 1¼ in. (3cm) seam allowance to the mattress width and twice the depth. This gives a generous tuck-under allowance so the sheet does not slip off the mattress easily.

2. Lay the fabric onto a flat surface and at each corner, using a marker pen or tailor's chalk, mark along each edge (from the corner point) the mattress depth and half the tuck-under allowance (5⅛ in. [13cm]). Use a metal rule or set square and tailor's chalk or marker pen to make a right angle from the side marks, and join the lines together.

3. Fold the fabric with wrong sides together, matching the lines and marks, and pin forming a dart. Stitch ⅜ in. (1cm) on the dart side of the line. Trim any excess fabric to ¼ in. (6mm) from the stitching line and refold the fabric with right sides together. Pin and stitch, taking ⅜ in. (1cm) seam allowance, forming a French seam (see page 55).

4. Alternatively, if a serger or overlocker is to be used, fold the fabric with right sides facing and pin on the marked line. Stitch and trim any excess fabric to ½ in. (1.3cm). Serge the edges.

5. Fold under and pin a double ⅝ in. (1.5cm) hem all around the edge of the sheet. To insert the elastic, leave a small gap of ⅝ in. (1.5cm) in the hem. Measure 10 in. (25cm) from the corners along the length of the sheet and mark the positions for the gaps. Stitch the hem edges, leaving the marked gaps.

6. Attach the safety pin to the elastic and feed through the slot. Adjust the gathering until the correct measurement is achieved and secure the pin. Cut the elastic and stitch at both ends to secure. Repeat on the other end of the sheet.

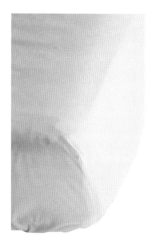

Elasticated corners ensure a snug fit over the mattress.

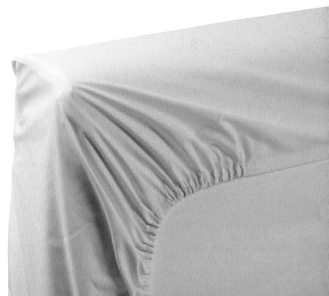

Pillowcases

Pillowcases can easily be made from sheeting fabric to combine with your bedding colors, or printed cottons can be used to add interest or contrast with the bedroom décor. Standard pillowcases are made to fit pillows 30 x 20 in. (75 x 50cm).

SKILL LEVEL
• 1

TOOLS
• Scissors
• Soft tape measure
• Sewing kit

MATERIALS
• Sheeting or suitable washable fabric
• Thread

SEE ALSO
• Fabric characteristics, p38
• Machine stitches, p51
• Seams and hems, p54

Plain or housewife pillowcase

This is the most popular style of pillowcase and is also the easiest to make.

1. This pillowcase can be cut in one piece: twice the length of the pillow plus 11 in. (28cm) and the width plus 1¼ in. (3cm). Cut the fabric, taking care to follow the straight grain (see page 38).

2. On one of the short ends, make a double fold (toward the wrong side) of ¼ in. (6mm). Pin and then machine stitch close to the edge. On the other short end, fold under ½ in. (1.3cm) and then 2 in. (5cm). Pin and stitch close to the edge. This wider hem will give a stylish finish on the front of the pillowcase. At this stage, you can stitch an embroidered design onto the hem or add a satin stitch in a contrast color to the stitching line for a decorative finish.

measurements NOTE
Although there is a standard pillow size, it is advisable to work from the measurements of the pillow you want to cover.

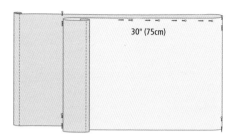

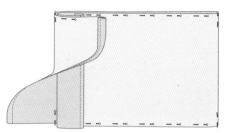

3. Place the fabric onto a flat surface and, with right side uppermost, mark with a pin or make a small snip in the edge of the fabric, 30 in. (75cm) and then another 30 in. (75cm) from the front side edge. Repeat on the other long edge. Fold over from the first mark to match with the second mark and pin the edges with right sides together, taking ⅝ in. (1.5cm) seam allowance.

4. Fold over the flap 8 in. (20cm) and make a crease with your fingers. Remove the pins from underneath the flap and then pin all the layers together.

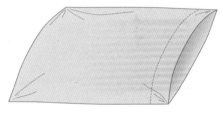

5. Stitch on the sewing machine, taking ⅝ in. (1.5cm) seam allowance. To neaten the edges, zigzag on the sewing machine or use a serger or overlocker.

6. Turn right side out, press, and gently push out the corners. This pillowcase provides an envelope effect to hold the pillow in.

This wide hem edge could be decorated with embroidery.

Oxford-style pillowcase

This pillowcase is made with an attached flange or border, 2 in. (5cm) wide.

SKILL LEVEL
• 1

TOOLS
• Scissors
• Soft tape measure
• Sewing kit

MATERIALS
• Sheeting or suitable washable fabric
• Thread

SEE ALSO
• Fabric characteristics, p38
• Machine stitches, p51
• Seams and hems, p54

1. This pillowcase is made from three pieces of fabric. For the front and back, add 5 in. (12.5cm) all around to the size of the pillow. Cut the back flap 11 in. (28cm) in length and add 5 in. (12.5cm) to the width. Cut the pieces, taking care to follow the straight grain (see page 38).

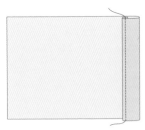

2. On one short edge of the back piece, fold under (toward the wrong side) ½ in. (1.3cm) and then 2 in. (5cm). Pin and stitch close to the edge.

3. On the back flap, make a double fold (toward the wrong side) of ¼ in. (6mm) on one long edge. Pin and machine stitch close to the edge.

4. With right sides together, pin the front and back pieces together, taking ⅝ in. (1.5cm) seam allowance. The back piece will reach up to 2½ in. (6.5cm) from the side edge.

5. Place the raw edge of the back flap onto this edge, right sides together. Pin this edge and then, removing the pins from underneath, pin through all the layers, along the sides.

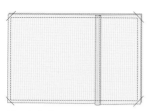

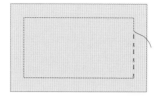

6. Stitch all around the pillowcase. Trim the corners off close to the stitching line. Press the seams open as far as possible into the corners and then turn right side out. Press again, gently pushing out the corners. It is easier to produce a crisp edge by pressing the seam open first.

7. Measure in 2 in. (5cm) from the edge of the pillowcase and pin together to mark the stitching line.

This non-frilled border gives a clean, chic finish.

8. The line can be basted, if preferred, or stitched on the sewing machine. Stitch again next to the first stitching line to strengthen and add detail. You can use satin stitch on top of the first stitching line, possibly in a contrasting color to coordinate with your bedroom décor. When stitching the border, take care not to stitch over the back flap, which must remain loose.

Bed skirts

Bed skirts are placed underneath the mattress and reach to the floor, covering the base of the bed. They are usually made from sheeting but can be made from curtain fabric, as they do not require such frequent laundering as the rest of the bed linen.

SKILL LEVEL
• 1

TOOLS
• Scissors
• Soft tape measure
• Sewing kit

MATERIALS
• Sheeting or curtain fabric
• Thread

SEE ALSO
• Fabric characteristics, p38
• Machine stitches, p51
• Seams and hems, p54
• Hand stitches, p42

technique NOTE
If the selvage is tight, you will need to remove it and use a French seam to join the widths together (see page 55). In this case, place the wrong sides together, pin, and stitch a ¼ in. (6mm) seam. Turn, pin, and stitch the right sides together, taking ⅜ in. (1cm) seam allowance. At the ends of the skirt, fold under ¼ in. (6mm) twice and stitch close to the edge.

Double skirt with box pleats

The skirt of the bed skirt can be box pleated, and the most stylish effect is achieved with box pleats on the corners and halfway along the edges. If you use curtain fabric, this is the most suitable design as it is less bulky than a gathered skirt.

1. Measure the base of the bed and add ⅝ in. (1.5cm) all around. For the skirt, measure to the required length and add 3 in. (7.5cm). For the width, measure the two long sides, one short side and 6–8 in. (15–20cm) at each side of the headboard end. To this add the pleats—five full pleats and two half pleats at the headboard. The optimum measurement for the box pleats is 16 in. (40cm).

2. Following the grain (see page 38), cut the required number of widths for the skirt and base. Use a plate to round off the corners of the base fabric. Check that the shape is correct, cut, and repeat on all the corners. Mark the center of the corner. Fold the fabric into four and mark the center points on each side.

3. With right sides facing, join the skirt sections together. Press the seams open, snipping into the selvage if necessary.

design NOTE
As the main part of the bed skirt is hidden under the mattress, it can be made from plain sheeting.

8" (20cm)

Basting stitches

4. Press up 2½ in. (6.5cm) at the hem toward the wrong side. Turn under ½ in. (1.3cm). Pin and stitch close to the edge, taking care not to twist the hem. Baste or insert pins at right angles to the hem line and remove them just before the machine needle reaches them.

5. Mark the center point of the skirt. With the fabric right side facing upward, make the first pleat. Mark 8 in. (20cm) either side of the center mark at the top and hem the edges of the skirt. Fold in toward the center, pin the top and bottom edges, then baste (see page 44).

6. Measure to the next pleat position (from the center of the base to the center of the curved corner). Mark this measurement on the skirt and then two marks of 8 in. (20cm). Fold to the center as before, pin, and baste. Check that the pleat is in the correct position.

7. Repeat this process along the side of the bed. At the headboard it is only necessary to use a half pleat and you can adjust the pleat size if necessary. The skirt needs to extend 6–8 in. (15–20cm) toward the center of the back.

8. Repeat this process on the other side of the skirt. With right sides together, pin the skirt to the base, matching up the marks. At the corners, snip into the center of the box pleat fabric to allow it to stretch, and pin. Place the fabric onto the bed base to check that it fits. If necessary, you can adjust each pleat to fit rather than unpin the entire length.

9. Stitch on a sewing machine, taking ⅝ in. (1.5cm) seam allowance. Zigzag or serge the edges. Press the edges toward the base and place under the mattress.

Gathered bed skirt

A gathered bed skirt is less formal than a box pleated one and can be made from sheeting or curtain fabric.

SKILL LEVEL
• 1

TOOLS
• Scissors
• Soft tape measure
• Sewing kit

MATERIALS
• Sheeting or curtain fabric
• Thread

SEE ALSO
• Fabric characteristics, p38
• Machine stitches, p51
• Seams and hems, p54

1. Measure the base of the bed and add ⅝ in. (1.5cm) all around. For the skirt, measure to the required length and add 2½ in. (6cm). For the width, measure the two long sides, one short side and add 6–8 in. (15–20cm) for each side of the headboard. Double this measurement to achieve the correct gathered effect.

2. Cut the required number of widths for the skirt, taking care to follow the grain (see page 38). At the corners of the base piece of fabric, use a plate to mark a curve to round off the corner. Check that the shape is correct and cut. Copy this shape on all four corners. Fold the fabric into four and mark the center points on each side with a pin, or make a small snip ⅛ in. (3mm) into the fabric, or use a marker pen.

3. With right sides facing, join the skirt sections together. Press the seams open. If the selvage is tight, you should remove it and use a French seam to join the widths together (see page 55). In this case, place the wrong sides together, pin, and stitch a ¼ in. (6mm) seam. Turn, pin, and stitch the right sides together, taking ⅜ in. (1cm) seam allowance. At the ends of the skirt, fold under ¼ in. (6mm) twice and stitch close to the edge to form a hem.

A gathered bed skirt in a bold color is a striking way to hide the base of the bed.

4. Make a double 1 in. (2.5cm) fold on the bottom edge, pin, and stitch, basting first if you prefer. Take care not to twist the hem. Pin at right angles and carefully remove the pins just before the machine needle reaches them.

5. Divide the skirt into four sections and make a double row of gathering stitches at the top of each section. Pull up the threads to fit the required measurement and secure by winding them around a pin. Repeat on all sections. With right sides together, pin to the main fabric, matching up the marks. The gathering reaches 6–8 in. (15–20cm) around the back edge of the base.

6. Stitch, taking ⅝ in. (1.5cm) seam allowance. Stitch again ¼ in. (6mm) into the seam allowance to add strength.

7. Either zigzag on the sewing machine or serge the edges together to neaten.

8. Press the seam upward toward the plain piece of fabric.

Table linen

Making your own table linen gives you the opportunity to use your choice of fabric, perhaps to coordinate with the rest of the kitchen or the dining room chairs.

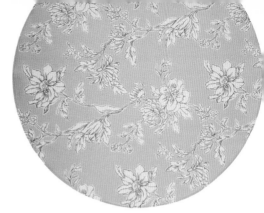

Tablecloths

One of the main considerations to bear in mind when making your own tablecloth is its intended purpose. Is it to cover up an ugly or old table standing in the corner of the room? Or is it to be used in a busy kitchen where it may require regular washing? Or perhaps it's for a plush dining table where guests will be entertained. Obviously, these different situations will require different qualities of fabric.

CALCULATING FABRIC

Unless you are making a fitted tablecloth, try to use a fabric that is wide enough not to require seams. If this is not possible, at least avoid having a central seam—instead, sew a strip of fabric to each side of a wider central panel. This applies to circular tablecloths as well as square, rectangular, and oval ones, though it shouldn't be a problem with narrower table runners.

• **Cloths for occasional, bedside, and dressing tables** are often layered, with the underneath layer floor length, or even a little longer so that it pools onto the floor.

• **Cloths for dining tables or kitchen tables,** however, should have an overhang of no more than 6–12 in. (15–30cm), so that the cloth does not get in the way of diners. The hem measurement, folded and machine stitched, is usually a double ½ in. (1.3cm). Hems can be bound with a contrast binding, decoratively serged (overlocked), or trimmed with lace or fringing.

Radius

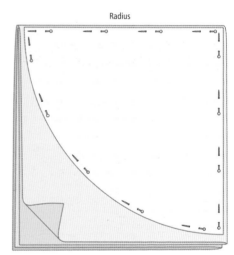

Cutting plan for circular tablecloth

Use this cutting plan to make the Circular tablecloth shown on page 168. Fold the fabric into four. Pin on the paper pattern and then cut through all the layers.

Placemats

Placemats can be any shape, and the size is down to personal preference: they can be round and just big enough to fit a plate, or they can be oval, rectangular, or square and large enough to hold cutlery too.

As with tablecloths, there are many options when it comes to adding trims or borders. Contrast borders are particularly attractive, and frills would give a country-kitchen look. Ribbon or braid trim are a more sophisticated option for special-occasion tableware.

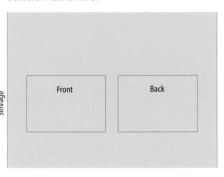

Selvage

Front

Back

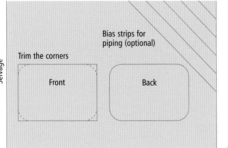

Selvage

Bias strips for piping (optional)

Trim the corners

Front

Back

Cutting plan for placemats

Use these cutting plans to make the projects shown on pages 172–174. Make sure you mark or pin the pieces to suit the pattern repeat, if applicable.

Napkins

Though small and simple, napkins can add to the impact of your dining table, so it is worth devoting a little thought to their design. Plain napkins can be made by making narrow or rolled hems on fabric squares. A contrast border in the same type of fabric adds interest without affecting washability.

QUILTING

Quilting in items such as tablemats provides the necessary thickness for the purpose of protecting a table surface. It is not, however, a heat protector on its own. Polyester batting or interlining is sandwiched between two layers of fabric. It is basted together and then the quilting design is marked onto the fabric. (See page 174 for instructions on how to make quilted placemats.)

Diagonal or square quilting is usually stitched on the sewing machine using a medium-length straight stitch. A walking foot (or even-feed foot) can be used to prevent puckering. Quilting is also useful when making bed covers, but this is on a much larger scale.

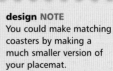

design NOTE
You could make matching coasters by making a much smaller version of your placemat.

Tablecloths

Tablecloths can be put to both decorative and functional use—blending colors together in a furnishing scheme while protecting the table beneath.

Square tablecloth with mitered corners and folded hem

Cottons and cotton mixes, and even sheeting, can be used where the cloth is regularly laundered. In more formal settings, thicker furnishing fabrics can be used and a glass cover or overcloth can be employed to protect the fabric.

SKILL LEVEL
• 1

TOOLS
• Scissors
• Soft tape measure
• Sewing kit

MATERIALS
• Fabric
• Thread

SEE ALSO
• Fabric characteristics, p38
• Seams and hems, p54
• Machine stitches, p51
• Hand stitches, p42

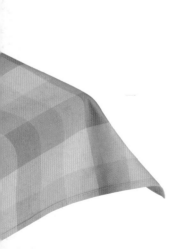

measurements NOTE
See page 164 for details on measuring fabric for tablecloths.

1. Measure the table and add twice the overhang plus 2½ in. (6.5cm) seam allowance. Cut the fabric, taking care to follow the grain line (see page 38).

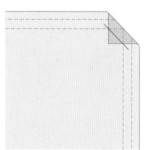

2. Make a double fold of ⅝ in. (1.5cm) around the edge and press. To miter the corner, open out the folded fabric. Fold the fabric inward from the inner crease point. Trim the excess fabric and refold.

3. Pin and stitch close to the edge using the sewing machine. Ladder stitch the corners to neaten and secure (see page 45).

Rectangular tablecloth

This tablecloth is made in the same way as the square version opposite. If the fabric is not wide enough, you will need a second length. Cut the second piece in half lengthwise and join it to the outside edges of the center piece, matching the pattern if necessary. Have a full width in the center, and use a flat fell seam (see page 56) to join the fabrics. When the measurement is calculated, fold the fabric in half so the center panel is even (pin the two seams together), and then mark the required width. Cut and finish as for the square tablecloth.

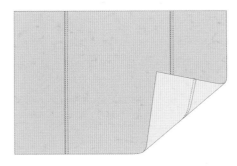

Oval tablecloth

This tablecloth is made in the same way as the rectangular version above. Join the fabric if necessary and cut it to the maximum width and length of the table, plus any overhang and allowances. Then:

1. Press the cloth and place it onto the table with an even amount hanging on all sides. Place weights on the table so the fabric does not move. Mark the hem exactly by measuring the overhang all the way around, indicating the line with pins or a marker pen. Trim off the excess fabric to create the oval shape. Stitch all the way around the edge of the cloth ½ in. (1.3cm) from the edge. ▼

3. Tuck the seam allowance under ¼ in. (6mm). Pin the hem every 6 in. (15cm) and then pin in between. This allows the fabric to sit smoothly without stretching.

4. If necessary, baste the hem before machine stitching or place pins at right angles to the hem and remove carefully just before the machine needle reaches them.

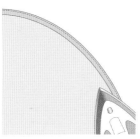

2. Press the edge in toward the wrong side, just allowing the stitching to be seen. This enables a smooth curve to be achieved.

Circular tablecloth

Circular tablecloths can look equally as good in a floral pattern at a short length or in a rich plain weave at floor length. They are made from a square of fabric cut to the correct measurement. This is achieved by adding the table diameter to twice the overhang depth required, plus 1 in. (2.5cm) seam allowance.

SKILL LEVEL
• 1

TOOLS
• Scissors
• Soft tape measure
• Sewing kit
• String and marker pen

MATERIALS
• Fabric
• Thread

SEE ALSO
• Rectangular tablecloth, p167
• Seams and hems, p54
• Machine stitches, p51

1. Cut the fabric and, if necessary, join as for the Rectangular tablecloth on page 167.

2. Fold the fabric into four, following the grain line or matching the fabric joins and place onto a flat surface. ▲

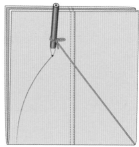

3. Attach the pen to the string and adjust to the correct length (half the diameter plus the seam allowance). Keeping the end of the string at the fold point, draw a line round the fabric to the required length.

4. Cut along this line, keeping all four layers together. If the fabric is too thick, cut the top one first and transfer the markings through to the next layer, then continue until all the layers are cut.

5. Unfold the fabric and place on the table to check that the length is correct (taking the seam allowance into consideration).

design NOTE
Circular tablecloths look more stylish when they reach the floor and hang better when lined.

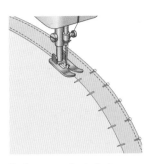

6. Stitch all the way around the edge of the cloth ½ in. (1.3cm) from the edge. Press the edge in toward the wrong side, just allowing the stitching to be seen. This allows a smooth curve to be achieved.

7. Fold under ¼ in. (6mm). Pin the hem every 6 in. (15cm) to start with and then pin in between. This allows the fabric to sit smoothly without stretching.

8. If necessary, baste the hem before machine stitching, or place the pins at right angles to the hem and remove carefully just before the machine needle reaches them. Remove any basting stitches and press.

The double hem is kept narrow so as not to interfere with the overall look of the tablecloth.

Lined, shaped table runner with tassel trim

Table runners are usually made from a narrow piece/width of fabric that runs the length of a table and are decorative rather than practical. They add a touch of color and glamor to a table set for dinner. They are often made from luxurious fabric and sometimes have a tassel trim.

SKILL LEVEL
• 1

TOOLS
• Scissors
• Soft tape measure
• Sewing kit
• Zipper foot

MATERIALS
• Fabric
• Lining
• Thread
• Two tassels

SEE ALSO
• Fabric characteristics, p38
• Hemming, p50
• Hand stitches, p36

1. Establish the size requirements of the runner. Place some fabric on the table to see what size gives the best appearance. It can drape over the edge of the table or sit along the center to feature a table decoration.

2. Add 1¼ in. (3cm) seam allowance to the maximum rectangular shape and cut out, taking care to follow the straight grain (see page 38) and to feature a pattern wherever possible. Cut the same size in lining or contrast fabric. Fold the fabric lengthwise and mark the desired shape using a ruler and marker pen. Open out, pin loosely, and confirm the correct shape. Adjust if necessary.

3. Cut along the marked line. Repeat for the lining.

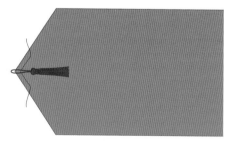

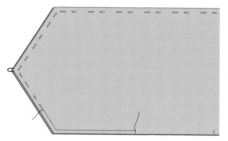

4. Place the hanging cord of the tassel to the points with the tassel facing inward, onto the right side of the fabric. Stitch the tassel using the zipper foot on the sewing machine, allowing ¼ in. (6mm) from the seam line to the head of the tassel.

5. Stitch to secure. With right sides together, pin the lining to the fabric, taking ⅝ in. (1.5cm) seam allowance. Leave a gap of 6 in. (15cm) along one of the straight long edges.

6. Stitch using the zipper foot on the sewing machine, pivoting on all the angles. Double stitch all the angles to reinforce.

LUXURIOUS FABRIC

To make a luxuriously sheer table runner, use a double layer of fabric instead of lining. Make up, following the instructions above. If necessary, cut the tassel cord if it is visible. To stop the cord fraying, use a touch of fabric glue or similar adhesive. When pressing sheer fabrics, keep the iron temperature low.

7. Graduate the seam allowance (see note on page 55) and trim off the corners. Do not cut the tassel cords. Before turning through to the front, press the seams open on the straight edges as far as possible, as this helps to produce a crisp edge when the fabric is pressed on the right side.

8. Turn right side out, gently pushing out the corners and pulling the tassel into place. Press carefully. Pin the opening together and stitch using a slip stitch.

BEADED TRIM

To make a simple rectangular runner finished off with a beaded trim, fold over the tape that secures the beads to neaten, then stitch it onto the top layer of the runner with the zipper foot attachment of the sewing machine. Pin the second layer to the top, right sides together, and stitch all around using the zipper foot, taking care not to catch any of the beads when stitching and leaving a 6 in. (15cm) gap at the bottom edge. Turn through and finish as before.

The tassel is sewn between the fabric and lining to make the runner reversible.

Placemats

Individual placemats are an attractive alternative to a tablecloth for protecting the table, or can be used in conjunction with a cloth. Curtain fabric or printed cottons can be used, but they must be washable.

SKILL LEVEL
• 1

TOOLS
• Scissors
• Soft tape measure
• Sewing kit

MATERIALS
• Fabric
• Interlining
• Thread

SEE ALSO
• Hand stitches, p42
• Machine stitches, p51

Rectangular placemat with Oxford-style edging

This is a simple design suitable for everyday use and will hold cutlery as well as a plate.

1. Cut out two pieces of fabric and one of interlining, 1¼ in. (3cm) larger than the finished measurement of 15 x 12 in. (45 x 30cm).

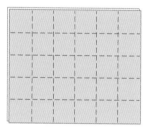

2. Place the interlining onto a flat surface and position one piece of fabric on top, right side upward. Baste together with large stitches working from the center outward, every 3–4 in. (7.5–10cm) (see page 44). Repeat in the other direction.

3. With right sides together, pin to the back piece, leaving a gap of 4 in. (10cm) in the center of the bottom edge. Stitch on the machine, taking ⅝ in. (1.5cm) seam allowance, pivoting at the corners. Stitch over the corners, again to add strength.

4. Trim the interlining close to the stitching line and graduate the other seam allowances (see note on page 55). Trim off the corners close to the stitching.

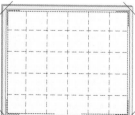

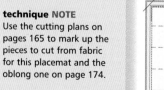

technique NOTE
Use the cutting plans on pages 165 to mark up the pieces to cut from fabric for this placemat and the oblong one on page 174.

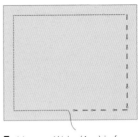

5. Turn right side out, taking care not to split the stitching at the edge of the gap. Gently push out the corners with a pointed instrument.

6. Press the edges and pin the opening together. Stitch together using a slip stitch and double-thread to add strength. Remove the basting stitches carefully.

7. Measure 1½ in. (4cm) in from the edge and mark with a line of pins. Stitch this line on the sewing machine, removing the pins as you reach them, or it can be basted first if you prefer.

This placemat can be used on either side.

Oblong quilted placemat with bound edge

Placemats can be layered with interlining, batting, or a thermal curtain lining to increase heat protection, and quilted in diagonal or square designs.

1. Cut out two pieces of fabric and one of interlining or batting 1 in. (2.5cm) larger than the finished measurement.

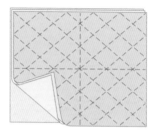

2. Sandwich the interlining between the two layers of fabric, matching up the edges. Pin and baste through the centers and then every 2–3 in. (5–7.5cm).

3. Decide on the distance between the lines of quilting and mark the first one between the opposite corners. Use either tailor's chalk and a ruler to mark the lines or the quilting bar attachment on the sewing machine to follow the stitching lines. Repeat this process in the other direction. When stitching the lines, take care not to stretch or pucker the fabric.

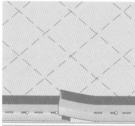

4. Place a saucer or small plate face down onto the corner, matching the edges of the plate with the edge of the fabric. Draw around the shape and remove the plate. Cut and repeat on the other corners by folding the mat so that all the curves are the same. Trim any loose threads.

5. Open out one edge of the bias tape and place the crease ½ in. (1.3cm) in from the edge, starting in the middle of the longest edge. Pin along this line, easing the tape around the corners. Overlap the tape edges by ½ in. (1.3cm) and fold the underneath end to enclose the raw edges.

6. Stitch on the crease line. Turn the placemat over and fold the tape to cover the stitching line. Pin and stitch on the sewing machine.

Napkins

Napkins can be made from a variety of washable fabrics. Napkins are usually finished off with a double ¼ in. (6mm) folded hem, or they can be decoratively finished off with the use of a serger or overlocker.

Square napkin

Napkins vary from 8 in. (20cm) to 20 in. (50cm) in size.

1. Cut a square of fabric 1 in. (2.5cm) larger than the finished required measurement, taking care to cut along the grain line (see page 38).

2. Make a double fold of fabric on each edge, ¼ in. (6mm) wide. Press.

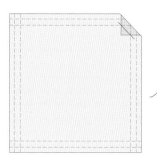

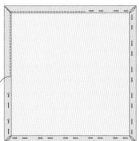

3. Open out the corner and fold inward from the inner corner point. Trim off the excess fabric and refold the creases inward.

4. Pin around all the edges and machine close to the hem edge, starting in the center of one of the sides and pivoting at the corners. Finish off the thread neatly and press. Use a ladder stitch (see page 45) to neaten the inside of the mitered corner.

SKILL LEVEL
• 1

TOOLS
• Scissors
• Soft tape measure
• Sewing kit

MATERIALS
• Fabric
• Thread

SEE ALSO
• Fabric characteristics, p38
• Machine stitches, p51
• Hand stitches, p42

DECORATIVE STITCHING

For an interesting effect, work a decorative machine stitch around the edge on the front side of the napkin using a contrast thread.

To achieve a fringed effect, top stitch around the napkin ½ in.(1.3cm) in from the edge and ravel the threads up to this line.

On plain linen and cotton napkins, embroider designs either on the machine or by hand.

Decorative details

All home décor projects—curtains, shades, tiebacks, valances, pelmets, pillows, bed linen, and table linen—can be adorned with extra detail. It is, however, important that the detail enhances the overall design, and this section shows you how a variety of attractive trimmings can do just that.

What works where

Adding decorative details and finishing touches to curtains, shades, pillows, valances, and tiebacks will complete the intended outcome of your home décor projects. They can range from simple piped edgings to elaborate frills, either gathered or pleated, a stylish border on the edge of a Roman shade or curtain, a contrasting border on the lower edge of a valance, or pin tucks on pillows and quilting.

Decorative details can be made from matching fabrics and stunning contrasts that coordinate with other fabrics and colors in the room to unify the whole look you are trying to achieve. As fabric accessories are smaller than the overall window treatment, they provide an ideal opportunity to add contrasting color, texture, or pattern. Plain curtains can be given an attractive edge with colored or patterned trimming in the form of braid, piping, or banding. Lace edging softens crisp cotton shades; corded fringes set off the pile of velvet.

Trimmings can also be used to adjust shape and proportion. The position of tiebacks, for example, will define the silhouette of curtains and hence affect the amount of light a room receives. Fringe applied to the lower edge of valances or curtains accentuates vertical lines and provides a sense of movement.

There are many types of decorative detail and many variations within each type, and, with a bit of imagination, you could come up with your own unique ideas.

Loops of coordinating cream and blue ribbon have been sewn onto this pillow, with the stitching cleverly concealed under an integrating strip of cream braid.

Fringes with short, brush-like or tasseled edging are typical of English Victorian décor and are inherently opulent. Today, they can be used effectively to complement period styles and to add movement to window treatments. More contemporary beaded or glass-drop fringes add a pretty touch of glamor. Such trimming can either be glued in place or sewn on the edge of the fabric. This type of decoration often suits transparent or lightweight draperies and has the practical advantage of helping the material to hang better.

Ribbon and braid come in a wide range of patterns, widths, and colors; some incorporate loops or scallops that add to the textural effect. Like upholstery braid, the type used for window treatments provides a neat finishing touch, lending crispness and definition. Colored braid is a useful way of adding interest to plain curtains or shades.

Piping and decorative cord are great ways to finish the edges of tiebacks, pillows, and many other home décor projects. They stylishly accentuate edges while giving a neat end result and can add dimension to an otherwise flat shade. It is possible to buy prepared piping in a small variety of colors, but it is easy to make your own from matching or contrasting fabric. It is important to select a suitable fabric to cover piping cord as fabrics that are very thin will not hide the structure of the piping cord and will also deteriorate rapidly.

Tassels are the punctuation points of window treatments and tend to be used in combination with corded rope to serve as tiebacks. They come in a huge range of sizes and styles and are often made of silk. Single tassels can be added to pillow corners for extra detail.

Beaded fringe

Twisted cord

Tasseled fringe

Gathering and frills

Gathering fabric is a simple way of adding a flounce to the edge of a pillow, tieback, or the lower edge of an Austrian shade. Gathering is also used on bed skirts and round pillows.

SKILL LEVEL
• 1

TOOLS
• Scissors
• Soft tape measure
• Metal tape measure
• Sewing kit

MATERIALS
• Fabric
• Thread

SEE ALSO
• Fabric characteristics, p38
• Machine stitches, p51

1. Cut the required number of widths across the fabric, following the pattern repeat if necessary and following the straight grain (see page 38).

2. Join the widths together with right sides facing, taking 1 in. (2.5cm) seam allowance, or match the pattern if required. This forms a circle of frill.

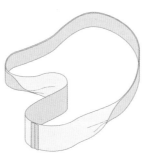

3. Trim the seam allowance or snip the selvage as required. Press the seams open and fold in half lengthwise.

4. If the frill is for a pillow, divide the frill into four sections and mark with a pin or snip the seam allowance.

5. Mark the center of the four sides on a square pillow. A round pillow will be folded into four and marked in the same way.

A tightly gathered frill gives the best effect.

measurements NOTE
Double fullness will give a generous frill. If there is enough fabric, a double frill is preferred and will not show a machined hem on the edge.

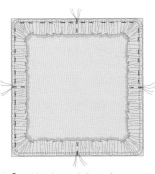

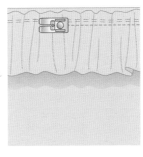

6. With a long stitch on the sewing machine, make two rows of gathering stitches between the quarter marks (see page 53). Pull up the gathers and place onto the pillow front, matching up the markers. Adjust the gathers to fit (allowing plenty of fullness at the corners) and wind the threads around a pin to secure.

7. Machine stitch just inside the gathering threads (so the threads will be inside the seam allowance), removing the pins as you reach them, or baste first if preferred.

technique NOTE

If the frill is for an Austrian shade, stitch the necessary panels together. To finish the ends, fold the fabric lengthwise with right sides together and machine stitch across the end, taking 1 in. (2.5cm) seam allowance. Trim to ½ in. (1.3cm) and trim off the corner. Turn through to the right side, press, and then gather into sections. Attach to the lower edge of the shade.

PLEATS

A pleated trim is made in the same way as a gathered frill, but requires a little more fabric. It is often used on the lower edge of a tieback, so only small quantities of fabric are required. For light- to mediumweight fabrics small pleats will be suitable, but for thicker fabrics larger pleats should be made. Box pleats often feature on bed skirts (see pages 160–161).

Tucks and pin tucks

Tucks are stitched folds of fabric that can be sewn singly or in multiples to add decoration. They can vary in width and very narrow tucks are called pin tucks. Use tucks to decorate pillows, pillowcases, and duvet covers. Light- to mediumweight cottons and polycottons produce the best results.

SKILL LEVEL
• 1

TOOLS
• Scissors
• Soft tape measure
• Metal tape measure
• Yard stick or ruler
• Sewing kit

MATERIALS
• Fabric
• Thread

SEE ALSO
• Machine stitches, p51
• Thread

1. When cutting the fabric, allow ¼–½ in. (6–13mm) for each tuck, depending on the size required.

2. Mark the position of the first tuck on the front side of the fabric using a yard stick or ruler. For continuous ¼ in. (6mm) tucks, make the next mark ¾ in. (2cm) away. Repeat until the required number of tucks has been indicated.

3. Fold the fabric, with wrong sides together, along the marker line, pin, and sew with a straight stitch on the sewing machine (see page 51). Stitch all the tucks in the same direction to avoid twisting the fabric. Finish the ends securely. A lustrous machine embroidery floss or a decorative stitch can be used to add to the detail.

4. Pin tucks can be positioned at chosen regular intervals and will require a stitching line ⅛ in. (3mm) from the fold. Press the tucks toward one direction, using a pressing cloth.

The tucks add detail to a plain pillow.

Contrast border edging

Contrast edging adds width or length to your curtains or shades, along with the perfect opportunity to add an accent to your color scheme. The chosen fabric needs to be of a similar weight so that it hangs correctly. It must also be cut from a single length of fabric so there are no joins. When combining fabrics it is a good idea to steam press them first to avoid different shrinkage rates.

Inside-edge contrast curtain edging

A contrasting border sewn to the inside (leading) edge of curtains adds to the width of the fabric and looks stylish.

1. Cut a strip of fabric the same length as the main fabric (see Lined curtains, page 70). The width is determined by the desired outcome—2–4 in. (5–10cm) looks good on most curtains. The narrower width is suitable on shorter curtains but for full-length curtains, a bolder, wider border looks in better proportion. To cut the width, add ⅝ in. (1.5cm) seam allowance plus 2 in. (5cm) side turning allowance to the finished width of the border (do not include the selvage). Cut off the selvage on the leading edge of the main fabric.

2. With right sides together and starting from the bottom edge, pin the contrast fabric to the main fabric, taking ⅝ in. (1.5cm) seam allowance.

3. Machine sew, making sure the border fabric does not pucker or stretch. Press the seam open and continue to make up as for Lined curtains (see pages 70–73).

The continuous lining conceals the fabric joins.

design NOTE
This border edging looks attractive with eyelet curtains (see page 88).

SKILL LEVEL
• 1

TOOLS
• Scissors
• Soft tape measure
• Metal tape measure
• Sewing kit

MATERIALS
• Fabric
• Contrast fabric
• Thread

SEE ALSO
• Machine stitches, p51

Top or hem contrast curtain edging

A contrast edge at the top of the curtain can look equally stylish, particularly with eyelets. This method can also be used to lengthen curtains.

To prepare a contrast border for the top or lower edge of the curtains, cut the same number of widths of contrast fabric, allowing ⅝ in. (1.5cm) seam allowance for the join to the main fabric and 2 in. (5cm) for the top turning or 8 in. (20cm) for the hem.

SKILL LEVEL
• 1

TOOLS
• Scissors
• Soft tape measure
• Metal tape measure
• Sewing kit

MATERIALS
• Fabric
• Contrast fabric
• Thread

SEE ALSO
• Seams and hems, p54
• Machine stitches, p51

1. Join the widths together, taking the same seam allowance as for the main fabric, so the seams will appear in the same position.

2. Press the seams open and snip or trim the seam allowance if necessary.

3. With right sides facing, pin the contrast to the top edge of the curtain, matching the seams. If attaching to the lower edge, use the same method. Machine stitch and press the seams open.

4. Continue to make the curtain following the relevant instructions.

Contrast edging on a Roman shade

As with edging for curtains, it is important to select a suitable contrast fabric that will hang correctly.

SKILL LEVEL
• 2

TOOLS
• Scissors
• Soft tape measure
• Metal tape measure
• Sewing kit

MATERIALS
• Fabric
• Contrast fabric
• Thread

SEE ALSO
• Machine stitches, p51

Side edging strip

1. Decide on the finished width of the edging strips. Take ⅝ in. (1.5cm) seam allowance for the joins and 1½ in. (3.5cm) for the side turning.

2. With right sides together, pin the contrast fabric strips to the main fabric, starting at the lower edge and working up toward the top edge.

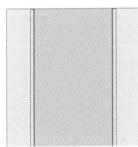

3. Machine stitch and press the seam open if the colors are similar. If there is a contrast, press the seam toward the darker fabric.

4. Continue to make the shade following the instructions on pages 107–109. When machine stitching the bottom pocket and the touch-and-close fastener, use a matching thread for the contrast edges on the bobbin of the sewing machine.

Lower edging strip

1. The most practical depth of strip is the depth of the bottom pocket, so that the machine stitching will disappear into the join of the contrast and main fabric. Cut 5 in. (13cm) by the width of the shade plus 3 in. (8cm). ▼

3. Continue to make the shade following the instructions on pages 107–109. On step 8, pin and stitch the bottom pocket from the right side of the fabric to follow the seam accurately.

2. With right sides together, pin the contrast to the lower edge of the fabric, taking ⅝ in. (1.5cm) seam allowance. Press the seam open or toward the darker fabric.

Trimmings

There are many different ways of decorating or updating your home décor with added trimmings. Ribbons, piping, fancy buttons, tassels, and beaded trims are all available in many different colors and styles. They can easily be added to existing items to update them or can be an integral part of the project.

SKILL LEVEL
• 1

TOOLS
• Scissors
• Soft tape measure
• Metal tape measure
• Sewing kit

MATERIALS
• Fabric
• Thread
• Ribbons
• Zipper, 4 in. (10cm) narrower than pillow width

SEE ALSO
• Cutting plans, p120
• Machine stitches, p51

Ribbon and braid

If you visit any sewing department you will find hundreds of different types of ribbon and braid, including velvet, satin, webbing, and organza to name but a few. They are available in many vibrant colors and widths, and can be sewn onto pillows to separate different fabrics, as ties, or at the top of sheer curtains to attach the top to the curtain pole.

Ribbon-decorated pillow

1. Cut the fabric pieces for your chosen pillow (see pages 120–123).

 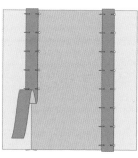

2. Stitch together the front pieces, press the seams open, and zigzag the edges.

3. Pin the ribbon or braid strips horizontally in place.

4. Machine down each side of the ribbon in the same direction to avoid twisting.

5. Continue to make up, following the relevant instructions.

Piping

There are many different thicknesses of piping cord, ranging from no. 1, usually used in dressmaking, to no. 6, which is a very thick example used in heavy home décor. No. 3 is medium size and can be used for most projects. It is a good size to use with home sewing machines with either a piping or zipper foot attachment. It is important to use a pre-shrunk piping cord. If this is not available, wash the cord before use.

Piping is used to define edges.

SKILL LEVEL
• 2

TOOLS
• Scissors
• Soft tape measure
• Metal tape measure
• Sewing kit
• Piping or zipper foot

MATERIALS
• Fabric
• Piping cord
• Thread

SEE ALSO
• Machine stitches, p51
• Hand stitches, p42
• Fabric characteristics, p38

To cut piping strips

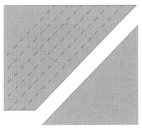

1. Fold the fabric to a 45-degree angle. This allows the piping to stretch and bend around corners, giving a smooth finish to pillows and tiebacks.

2. Cut through the fold and proceed to mark the strips on the larger piece of fabric.

To measure the width required

1. Use a soft tape measure to place round the cord and add ½ in. (1.3cm) seam allowance to stitch into the seam—1 in. (2.5cm) in total. If you are using no. 3 piping cord, strips of 1¾ in. (4.5cm) will be sufficient. If you are using a fabric that ravels badly, allow extra seam allowance that can be trimmed off after sewing.

2. Measure around the pillow or item to be piped to calculate how many strips will be required.

Pillow with piping

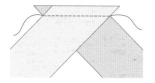

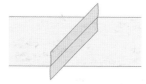

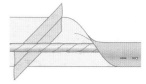

1. Join the strips together, with right sides facing and overlap ¼ in. (6mm).

2. Machine stitch (or back stitch by hand, see page 50). Press the seam open with your fingers.

3. Place the piping cord in the center of the wrong side, fold over, and pin together. Prepare enough to fit around the chosen item.

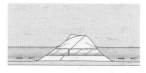

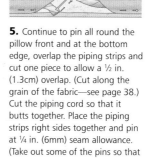

4. If you are piping a square pillow, start by placing the piping at the bottom center of the front piece. Match the edges together and use the pins from the piping to secure to the pillow front. Take care not to stretch the piping as it will return to its initial length and then cause puckering. The best way to avoid this is to lay the fabric on to a flat surface and allow the piping to follow the edge without stretching it. Take out a pin from the piping and place it through all the layers. As the piping has been cut on the bias it will bend round the corners. It may be necessary to snip the seam allowance of the piping if the fabric is very firm.

5. Continue to pin all round the pillow front and at the bottom edge, overlap the piping strips and cut one piece to allow a ½ in. (1.3cm) overlap. (Cut along the grain of the fabric—see page 38.) Cut the piping cord so that it butts together. Place the piping strips right sides together and pin at ¼ in. (6mm) seam allowance. (Take out some of the pins so that you are able to lift up the piping strips.) Stitch and press the seam open with your fingers.

6. Pin across the piping to complete and, using the zipper foot on the sewing machine, stitch all around the pillow close to the piping cord.

7. Complete the pillow, following the instructions on pages 124–125.

Attaching piping to a shade

1. Cut the piping cord to the finished length required and cut the piping strip ½ in. (1.3cm) longer.

2. Fold the piping strip tightly over the cord and pin together to give a sharp edge.

3. Pin in place and machine using the zipper foot. Complete the project following the relevant instructions.

Piping helps to conceal the zipper.

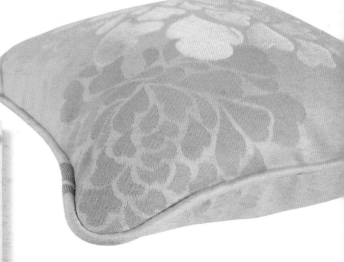

design NOTE
When piping with contrasting color, select a similar weight of fabric as the pillow to produce the best result.

Decorative cord

Decorative cord can be purchased with or without a flanged edging. For home sewing it is not a good idea to use the thickest flanged cords as they are difficult to attach. The cord can be stitched onto pillows after completion by hand but the flanged cords are sewn in as for piping cord.

1. Snip the corners as the flange tape is tight and will not bend around corners in the same way as bias strips. The joining process is also different. Overlap the cord by 2 in. (5cm) and unpick the stitching (the flange from the cord). Unravel the cords up to the joining point and entwine them. Pin together securely.

2. Using the zipper foot, stitch over the join. Stitch again, ¼ in. (6mm) into the seam allowance to secure all the loose ends. Continue to stitch all around the pillow. Trim any loose cords and zigzag over the ends (see page 52). Continue with the instructions for a Pillow with piping on page 188 to complete.

3. To hand stitch the cord onto a pillow, entwine together the separated cords and tuck into gaps in the machine stitching. Stitch over the gaps before completion.

FRINGING

There are many different designs of fringed edging. Tasseled and bobbled fringing can be added to pillows, valances, and the lower edge of Roman shades; traditional deeper fringing is usually added to the leading edges of long curtains and formal circular tablecloths. It is easier to add the fringed edging after the item is finished, except on the edge of pillows, where a neater finish is achieved when it is sewn in during construction, between the layers.

SKILL LEVEL
• 1

TOOLS
• Scissors
• Soft tape measure
• Metal tape measure
• Sewing kit
• Piping or zipper foot

MATERIALS
• Fabric
• Beaded trim
• Thread
• Optional contrasting fabric
  (paneled pillow only)

SEE ALSO
• Rectangular panel pillow,
  p187
• Machine stitches, p51

Beaded trim

This is a very popular trim and there are many designs and qualities available. It can be expensive, but a small amount stitched onto a pillow is a stunning addition. It can be stitched on the leading (inside) edge of a curtain or onto the lower edge of a Roman shade or valance. Tiebacks made from beads are also available.

Paneled pillow with beaded trim

1. Follow the instructions for the Rectangular panel pillow on page 134. On step 3, insert the beaded trim.

2. Pin the flanged edging onto the front panel, taking ⅝ in. (1.5cm) seam allowance. Stitch close to the edge of the tape using the zipper foot. Repeat on the other side of the front panel.

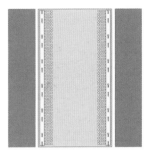

3. Using the zipper foot, pin and stitch the sides to the center panel, taking care not to stitch over the beads. Follow the instructions to complete the pillow.

Valance with beaded trim

For cutting out and preparing the fabric and lining, follow the instructions for the Lined valance with contrast or frilled trim (see page 100).

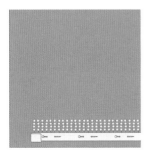

1. Pin the beaded trim onto the lower edge of the valance, taking ⅝ in. (1.5cm) seam allowance, starting 2 in. (5cm) in from the side edge. The tape must be folded over to conceal the raw edge before placement.

2. Machine, using the zipper foot close to the edge of the tape.

3. Continue from step 6 of the instructions for the Lined valance on page 100 to complete.

Tassels

Tassels are a fun way to embellish pillows, shades, table runners, and even cupboard door handles. There are many designs to choose from and most of the tassels available are part of a range of cords, fringing, and trimmings in many colors and qualities. They can easily be made from wool, silk yarn, or embroidery floss.

SKILL LEVEL
• 1

TOOLS
• Scissors
• Sewing kit
• Tapestry needle

MATERIALS
• Small pieces of cardboard
• Yarn
• Batting/cotton balls

Simple tassel

1. Cut two pieces of card to the desired length of the tassel. Place them together and wind one or more colors of the chosen yarn around the card at least 20 times (about 32 ft [10m] of yarn).

2. When the desired thickness is reached, slide a separate piece of yarn between the pieces of card and tie tightly in a knot around the loops of the yarn. Trim the ends and hide the knot inside the loops.

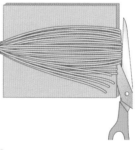

3. Slide the scissors' blade between the pieces of card and cut the loops at the other end. Remove the card.

4. If desired, pad the head of the tassel by pushing tiny pieces of batting or cotton wool inside. Bind one-fifth of the way down with a separate length of yarn.

5. Thread both ends of the binding yarn through a tapestry needle and take them through the top of the tassel at the center. Use these to attach the tassel to the project. A twisted cord can be inserted into the top of the tassel and used to attach to the project.

Ball tassel

This tassel is topped with a small ball (a wooden bead or polystyrene ball) covered with the chosen yarn. Decorative wooden or glass beads are effective and can be used as an alternative.

SKILL LEVEL
• 1

TOOLS
• Scissors
• Sewing kit
• Tapestry needle

MATERIALS
• Wooden bead or polystyrene ball
• Yarn
• Small pieces of cardboard

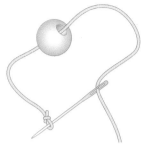

1. Ensure that the hole in the bead is sufficiently large to thread a tapestry needle through—it may be necessary to enlarge it with a knitting needle.

2. Thread a tapestry needle with the chosen yarn. Tie a small loop at the end of a long length of yarn (enough to cover the ball many times). Thread the needle through the ball or bead, then take it through the loop; pull tight.

3. Wind the yarn round and through the hole again. Repeat until the entire ball or bead is covered to the desired thickness. Fasten off on the underside.

4. Make a tassel from the same yarn, following the instructions opposite. After threading one of the ends of the binding, thread from the top of the tassel, through the ball, back down over the side of the ball, and inside the tassel. Repeat to secure. Repeat this process with the other binding thread and use the ends to secure to the project.

Design directory

Whether you want to achieve a look of luxury or are driven by more practical concerns, deciding on which style of curtain, shade, valance, or pillow to make can be difficult, as there are so many options available. This chapter explores various ideas that will help to find the perfect solution for your project and for your home.

Curtain designs

The main elements to consider that will affect the design of your curtains are the desired overall look, for example formal or informal, the décor and style of the room in which they are to hang, and the window they will be decorating.

Curtain length

The options are endless when it comes to curtain length, but there are some basic principles, both practical and stylistic, to bear in mind when making your choice. Generally, the longer the panel, the more formal the effect.

1 Sill-length curtains for a window in a recess or above furniture, or one opened frequently; ideal for kitchens and bathrooms as they are easier to clean than fuller-length curtains
Skill level Depends on heading used
Measurements Sill length
Fabric type All weights

2 Below-sill-length curtains
Skill level Depends on heading used
Measurements 4 in. (10cm) below the sill (or should sit just above a radiator)
Fabric type All weights

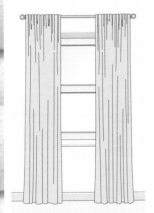  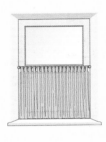

3 Floor-length curtains, elegant and stylish option for a living room
Skill level Depends on heading used
Measurements ½ in. (1cm) above the floor
Fabric type Sheer unlined curtains or lined curtains hang better with heavier fabric

4 Puddled curtains
Skill level Depends on heading used
Measurements Add another 5–6 in. (12.5–15cm) of fabric to floor length to achieve the puddling
Fabric type Medium- or heavyweight

5 Casual half-length café curtains, ideal for kitchens as they are easier to clean than fuller-length curtains
Skill level 1
Measurements Half sill-length
Fabric type Lightweight or sheer

see ALSO
• *Window treatments, pages 62–91*

design NOTE
Puddled curtains are not suitable for windows around which there will be a lot of traffic.

Window type

The type of window your curtains are intended to decorate will affect the style of curtain you choose. Bear in mind the opening mechanism and how accessible it needs to be. Also, assess the amount of light the window allows in to the room and how dressing the window in certain ways could change this.

BAY AND BOW WINDOWS

Bay windows form angled recesses, whereas bows form curved ones. Curtains may be hung outside the recess, with shades used to cover individual windows. Alternatively, curved or angled rods can be used to hang panels directly on the window frames.

see ALSO
• *Curtains, pages 62–91*
• *Tassels, pages 192–193*

design NOTE
Double-tracked draperies work most effectively when the inner curtain is in a contrasting or sheer fabric.

1 Three panels, for double window units
Skill level Depends on heading used
Measurements Floor length: ½ in. (1cm) above the floor
Fabric type Sheer unlined curtains or lined curtains hang better with heavier fabric

2 Four panels, for bay or bow window
Skill level Depends on heading used
Measurements Floor length: ½ in. (1cm) above the floor
Fabric type Sheer unlined curtains or lined curtains hang better with heavier fabric

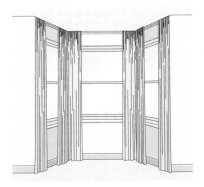

3 Multiple panels for optimized versatility at a bay window
Skill level Depends on heading used
Measurements Floor length: ½ in. (1cm) above the floor
Fabric type Sheer unlined curtains or lined curtains hang better with heavier fabric

4 Double-tracked draperies, for bow window
Skill level Depends on heading used
Measurements Floor length: ½ in. (1cm) above the floor
Fabric type Sheer unlined curtains or lined curtains hang better with heavier fabric

5 Curtains with tasseled tiebacks and a gathered valance running across front of recess, for bay with recess
Skill level Depends on heading used
Measurements Floor length
Fabric type Sheer unlined curtains or lined curtains hang better with heavier fabric

6 Rosette-trimmed shades with curtains outside the recess, for bay with recess
Skill level Depends on heading used
Measurements Add another 3–4 in. (7.5–10cm) of fabric to floor-length to achieve subtle puddling
Fabric type Heavyweight

DORMER WINDOWS

Since dormer windows are set within a recess projecting from the sloping plane of a roof, there's often insufficient wall space at either side to allow for standard curtains. Hinged or swivel rods are one solution. Another is to suspend the curtain outside the recess. Or, if you don't mind sacrificing a little light, short curtains can be fixed to the frame and softly pulled back to either side.

7 Fixed or tied-back lacy panels hanging outside the recess and tied back to the wall, for dormer window
Skill level 1
Measurements Halfway between sill and floor
Fabric type Lightweight

8 Rod-pocket curtains with tiebacks on swivel rods, for dormer window
Skill level 1
Measurements Sill length
Fabric type All weights

9 Ring-headed draperies held back by a pole, for dormer window
Skill level 1
Measurements Floor length: ½ in. (1cm) above the floor
Fabric type Lightweight

see ALSO
• Curtains, pages 62–91
• Tiebacks, pages 92–95

design NOTE
Use fixed curtains with a shade to block out the light.

French windows and sliding doors

Any treatment for French windows or sliding doors must allow easy passage. One solution is to suspend curtains high above the frame and extend the track or rod clear of it on either side so that the fabric does not get caught in the doors. Alternatively, the curtains themselves may be stationary, with lace panels, sheers, or shades installed on the doors.

10 Puddled silk curtains with toning foldover heading and tiebacks, for French windows/sliding doors
Skill level 2
Measurements Add another 5–6 in. (12.5–15cm) of fabric to floor length to achieve the puddling
Fabric type All weights

11 Casual floor-length curtains with individual jute Roman shades, for French windows/sliding doors
Skill level Depends on heading used
Measurements Floor length: ½ in. (1cm) above the floor
Fabric type Sheer unlined curtains or lined curtains hang better with heavier fabric

12 Asymmetric tab top curtain and fabric tieback, for French windows/sliding doors
Skill level 1
Measurements Floor length: ½ in. (1cm) above the floor
Fabric type All weights

13 Bowed valance and floor-length curtains, for French windows/sliding doors
Skill level 2
Measurements Floor length: ½ in. (1cm) above the floor
Fabric type Sheer unlined curtains or lined curtains hang better with heavier fabric

see ALSO
• Curtains, pages 62–91
• Tiebacks, pages 92–95
• Valances, pages 96–101

Choosing a heading

Your choice of heading will go a long way toward defining the style of your curtain. There is a wide range of options, from soft gathered styles to more formal tailored versions. A heading should be chosen with reference to the type of fabric as well as its pattern. Lightweight sheers suit informal gathered styles; heavier, more textured fabrics lend themselves to the crisp detail of pleating.

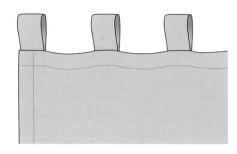

1 Tab top
Skill level 1
Measurements 1½ x window width
Fabric type Light- and mediumweight

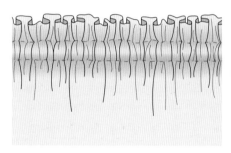

2 Ruffled rod pocket
Skill level 2
Measurements Double width of window
Fabric type Light- or mediumweight

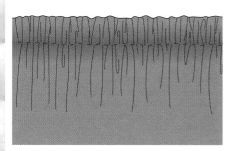

3 Plain rod pocket
Skill level 1
Measurements Double width of window
Fabric type Light- to mediumweight

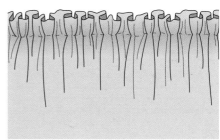

4 Gathered
Skill level 1
Measurements Double width of window
Fabric type All weights

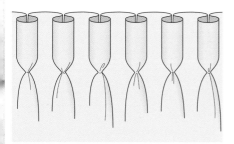

5 Goblet pleat
Skill level 3
Measurements Double width of window
Fabric type Medium- to heavyweight

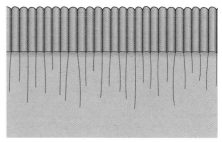

6 Pencil pleat
Skill level 1
Measurements 2½ times window width
Fabric type All weights

see ALSO
- *Tab top curtains, pages 74–77*
- *Other headings, pages 82–89*
- *Unlined curtains, pages 68–69*
- *Lined curtains, pages 70–73*

design NOTE
Pencil pleat tape is the most popular heading tape. It is available in various widths and is used on all curtain lengths. It also has a choice of pocket positions for the hooks.

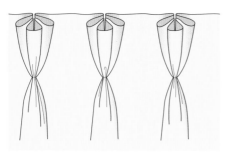

7 French or triple pleat
Skill level 3
Measurements Double width of window
Fabric type Medium- to heavyweight

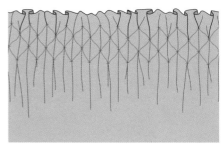

8 Smocked
Skill level 2
Measurements 2½ times width of window
Fabric type Light- to mediumweight

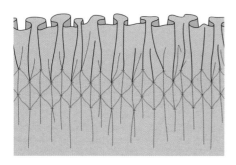

9 Smocked with ruffle
Skill level 2
Measurements 2½ times width of window
Fabric type Light- to mediumweight

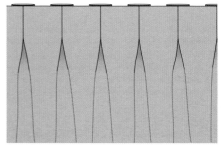

10 Inverted pleat
Skill level 3
Measurements Double width of window
Fabric type All weights

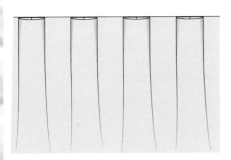

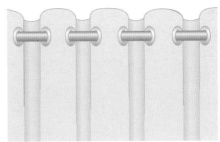

11 Box pleat
Skill level 3
Measurements 2½–3 times width of window
Fabric type All weights

12 Eyelet
Skill level 2
Measurements 1½ times width of window
Fabric type All weights

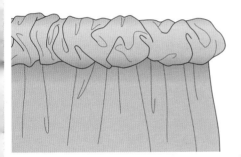

13 Puffed
Skill level 1
Measurements Double width of window + length of
frill x 2 + 1½ in. (4cm)
Fabric type Light- to mediumweight

see ALSO
- *Interlined curtains with
triple pleat heading,
pages 80–81*
- *Other headings,
pages 82–89*

measurements NOTE
The measurements given
in this section are for
guidance only. For more
accurate measurements,
please refer to the relevant
project earlier in the book,
where applicable.

Valance and pelmet designs

Valances and pelmets add interest to and dress the top of the window. They hide the necessary tracks and cords of curtains, but have a decorative function too.

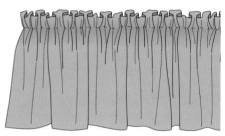

1 Pencil pleat
Skill level 1
Measurements 2½–3 times width of window
Fabric type All weights

2 Gathered pleat
Skill level 1
Measurements Double width of window
Fabric type All weights

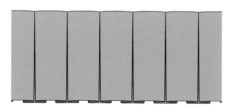

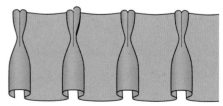

3 Inverted box pleat
Skill level 3
Measurements 2½ times width of window
Fabric type All weights

4 Pinch pleat
Skill level 3
Measurements Double the track width
Fabric type All weights

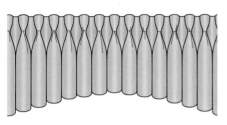

5 Pinch pleat with arch
Skill level 3
Measurements Double the track width
Fabric type All weights

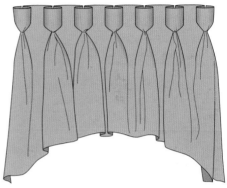

6 Goblet pleat
Skill level 3
Measurements Double the track width
Fabric type All weights

see ALSO
- *Lined valance with pencil pleat heading, pages 96–97*
- *Other headings, pages 82–89*
- *Lined valance with pinch pleat or goblet pleat heading, pages 98–99*

design NOTE
A valance can correct the proportions and, depending on where it is placed, it can visually shorten, lengthen, widen, or streamline a window. Pelmets will give the same results but are smoother, fixed structures.

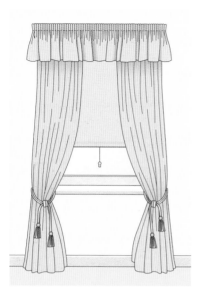

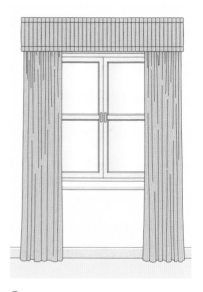

7 Pencil-pleated valance with matching floor-length curtains with tiebacks and roll-up shade
Skill level 1
Measurements Valance: 2½ times width of window; floor-length curtains: ½ in. (1cm) above the floor; shade: see Calculating fabric, page 104
Fabric type Sheer unlined curtains or lined curtains hang better with heavier fabric

8 Cushioned pelmet with matching floor-length curtains
Skill level 3
Measurements Pelmet: 2½–3 times width of window; floor-length curtains: ½ in. (1cm) above the floor
Fabric type Sheer unlined curtains or lined curtains hang better with heavier fabric

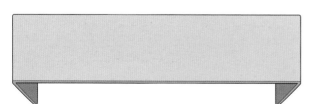

9 Straight-edged pelmet
Skill level 2
Measurements Required width plus depth on each side
Fabric type All weights

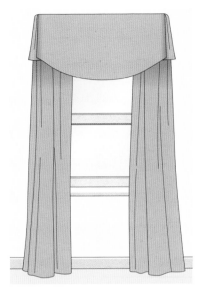

10 Tapestry-covered pelmet with Roman shade
Skill level 2
Measurements Pelmet: width of window + returns + seam allowance; shade: see Calculating fabric, page 104
Fabric type All weights

11 Curved pelmet with curtains
Skill level 3
Measurements Pelmet: width of window + returns + seam allowance
Fabric type Sheer unlined curtains or lined curtains hang better with heavier fabric

see ALSO
• *Lined valance with pencil pleat heading, pages 96–97*
• *Roll-up shades, page 113*
• *Tassels, pages 192–193*
• *Pelmets, pages 114–115*
• *Roman shades, pages 106–111*

Shade designs

The fabric shade is a great problem-solver. It allows you to make fine adjustments to both the amount of privacy and the degree of light a room receives because it can be lowered, raised, or made to sit at any level.

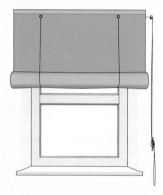

1 Roll-up
Skill level 1
Measurements See Calculating fabric, page 104
Fabric type Light- and mediumweight

2 Stagecoach
Skill level 2
Measurements To desired length at window plus roll-up section allowance
Fabric type Light- and mediumweight

see ALSO
• Roll-up shades, page 113
• Roman shades, pages 106–111
• Tiebacks, pages 92–95
• Valances, pages 96–101

design NOTE
As with curtains, you'll need to consider the appropriate style for the room, the practicalities of opening the window, and the function of the shade—for example, whether it's decorative or needed for privacy.

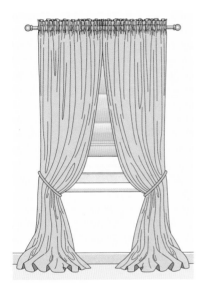

3 Interlined Roman shade with puddled tieback curtains

Skill level 3

Measurements Puddled curtains: add another 5–6 in. (12.5–15cm) of fabric to floor length; shade: see Calculating fabric, page 104

Fabric type Sheer unlined curtains or lined curtains hang better with heavier fabric; light- and mediumweight for the shade

4 Roman shade with tented curtains and matching valance and lining

Skill level 3

Measurements Puddled curtains: add another 5–6 in. (12.5–15cm) of fabric to floor length; shade: see Calculating fabric, page 104

Fabric type Sheer unlined curtains or lined curtains hang better with heavier fabric; light- and mediumweight for the shade

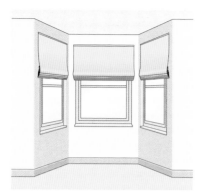

5 Roman shades at bay window
Skill level 1
Measurements See Calculating fabric, page 104
Fabric type Light- and mediumweight

6 Double Roman shade
Skill level 1
Measurements See Calculating fabric, page 104
Fabric type Light- and mediumweight

7 Single Roman shade with undressed sidelights
Skill level 1
Measurements See Calculating fabric, page 104
Fabric type Light- and mediumweight

8 Double shade with braided shaped hem
Skill level 2
Measurements Shade (see Calculating fabric, page 104) + shaped hem
Fabric type Light- and mediumweight

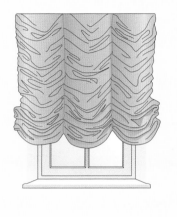

9 Cascade
Skill level 1
Measurements As Roman shades (see Calculating fabric, page 104), but the gap between the rod pockets decreases as you go up the shade
Fabric type Light- and mediumweight

10 Austrian
Skill level 2
Measurements Requires larger quantity of fabric for the flounces
Fabric type Sheer; printed cottons; taffeta

see ALSO
• Roman shades, pages 106–111
• Cascade shades, page 112
• Austrian shades, page 113

Pillow designs

Pillows can add the finishing touch to a room, livening up a sofa or lifting a tired décor. They can also serve a practical purpose—to make a chair more comfortable or to soften a garden bench.

1 Square
Skill level 1
Measurements Pad + ⅝ in. (1.5cm) seam allowance sides; pad + ¾ in. (2cm) seam allowance length
Fabric type All weights

2 Square with piped edge
Skill level 2
Measurements As Square, left, + ⅝ in. (1.5cm) seam allowance front, + ⅝ in. (1.5cm) side, + ¾ in. (2cm) bottom edge
Fabric type All weights

see ALSO
- *Square pillow, pages 124–125*
- *Square pillow with a piped edge, pages 126–128*
- *Oxford-style pillow, pages 132–133*
- *Rectangular panel pillow, pages 134–135*
- *Box cushion, pages 129–131*
- *Bolster with piped ends, pages 138–139*

design NOTE
A square pillow is the most popular shape and is also very versatile to work with as it can be decorated or edged in many ways, or simply left plain if the minimal style suits or if the fabric design is decorative enough on its own.

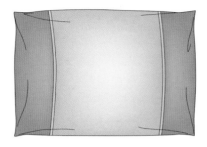

3 Oxford
Skill level 1
Measurements 1½–2 in. (4–5cm) border + ⅝ in.
(1.5cm) seam allowance at the front and ⅝ in.
(1.5cm) seam allowance at the sides on the back;
+ 1½ in. (4cm) for zipper or 1¾ in. (4.5cm) for
touch-and-close fastener length
Fabric type All weights

4 Rectangular panel pillow
Skill level 2
Measurements + ⅝ in. (1.5cm) seam allowance
on all pieces; lower edge + ¾ in. (2cm) seam
allowance on all pieces
Fabric type All weights

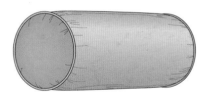

5 Square box
Skill level 2
Measurements Foam + ⅝ in. (1.5cm) seam
allowance all around. Front gusset: depth +
1¼ in. (3cm) seam allowance; back gusset—
zipper section: depth + 2¼ in. (5.5cm) seam
allowance. Front gusset measurement + back
gusset measurement = total gusset
measurement
Fabric type Washable and hardwearing

6 Bolster with piped ends
Skill level 1
Measurements Pad circumference + 1½ in. (3cm)
seam allowance; pad length + 1¼ in. (3cm);
end = radius + ⅝ in. (1.5cm)
Fabric type All weights

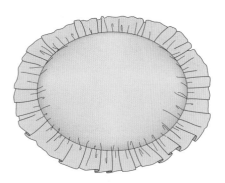

7 Round box
Skill level 2

Measurements Foam + ⅝ in. (1.5cm) seam allowance all around. Front gusset: depth + 1¼ in. (3cm); back gusset—zipper section: depth + 2¼ in. (5.5cm). Front gusset measurement + back gusset measurement = total gusset measurement

Fabric type Washable and hardwearing

8 Round with frill
Skill level 1

Measurements Back: pad diameter + ⅝ in. (1.5cm) seam allowance around the edge + 1½ in. (3cm) length (for zipper opening)

Fabric type All weights

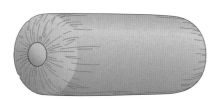

9 Bolster with gathered end and button detail
Skill level 1

Measurements Pad length + end diameter + 1½ in. (3cm) seam allowance

Fabric type All weights

10 Squab
Skill level 2

Measurements + ⅝ in. (1.5cm) seam allowance

Fabric type Washable and hardwearing

Many different styles of pillow can be grouped together to form an attractive—and comfortable—design feature. Be sure that the covers coordinate well though.

11 Cube
Skill level 1
Measurements + ⅝ in. (1.5cm) seam allowance
Fabric type Washable and hardwearing

see ALSO
- *Round pillow, pages 136–137*
- *Bolster with a gathered end and button detail, pages 140–141*

design NOTE
Squab cushions should be cut to the exact shape of the chair seat and are usually tied at the chair back.

Fabric directory

Choosing the right fabric for your project is crucial to its success. You might be driven primarily by color and/or design, but it is also important to consider the weight of the fabric and how this affects its suitability for your specific project and any aftercare that may be required.

Lightweight fabrics

Fabrics described as lightweight vary a great deal. Some may be light and soft (e.g. Thai silk), others light and crisp (e.g. organdy), while some may be strong (e.g. organza), or even sheer or transparent (e.g. voile). Lightweight fabrics are more suited to delicate finishes such as decorating windows and making pillows or bed linen. These fabrics are less appropriate for heavy-duty upholstery and functional curtains designed to insulate and keep out the light.

GENERAL ADVICE

- As 100 percent silk fabrics deteriorate in direct sunlight, it is important to line silk curtains or carefully consider their location.

- Use a fine, standard, or microtex needle (size 9 or 11) when sewing lightweight fabrics.

- Use a short to medium stitch length for sewing—i.e. 12 to 15 stitches per inch (2mm) or 10 stitches per inch (2.5mm).

- When sewing a lightweight fabric on a sewing machine, support the fabric in front of and behind the needle. This will help to prevent the seam from "crinkling" when finished.

- Iron seams flat before pressing them open and neatening the raw edges. This, in addition to the above tip, helps to limit the crinkling that sometimes occurs.

- It may be necessary to cut off the selvage before sewing the curtain panels together, and use a French seam (see page 55) to enclose all the raw edges.

- Use a straight-stitch presser foot or sole plate when sewing a straight stitch on a lightweight fabric. It is less likely that the fabric will be pushed down into the body of the machine.

- Lightweight fabrics are generally more delicate than heavier weights, so choose appropriate projects that will not get too much wear.

- Narrow seams are a good choice for sheer fabrics.

Sheer

Examples: Voile, organza, organdy, lace, broderie anglaise, net, tulle, cheesecloth.
Use for: Bed canopies, decorative drapes, shades.
Avoid: Heavy-duty upholstery, slipcovers, pillows (unless backed with a second, denser layer of fabric), and curtains designed for insulation and to keep out the dark.

Crisp

Examples: Organza, voile, organdy, net, tulle, taffeta, dupion.
Use for: Shades where volume is required, curtains/ drapes, or decorative pillows.
Avoid: Heavy-duty upholstered furniture, slipcovers.

Soft

Examples: Cheesecloth, cotton lawn, Thai silk.
Use for: Bed linen, pillows, informal curtains/drapes, table linen.
Avoid: Heavy-duty upholstered furniture, slipcovers, beanbags.

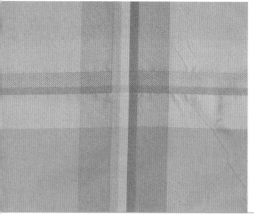

Silk plaid

Description: Silk fabric woven or printed in a plaid design.

Suitable use: Luxurious curtains, bed coverings, and decorative
pillows. The size of the plaid will influence the scale—i.e.
large windows will look better with a large plaid pattern.

Cutting/sewing: Be aware of matching the vertical and
horizontal stripes when cutting out. Use a walking foot
attachment on the sewing machine to reduce the "creep"
that occurs and so help match the pattern.

Care: Use a vacuum cleaner and brush nozzle on upholstery
and drapes, otherwise dry-clean. Silk will fade and deteriorate
in sunlight, so add a lining and avoid very sunny windows.

Cheesecloth

Description: Traditionally used to wrap cheese, this loosely
woven cotton cloth has a crinkled texture with a crêpe finish.

Suitable use: Soft drapes and shades are appropriate styles for
cheesecloth rather than sharp, formal designs. Use it for
dressing windows and for bed canopies.

Cutting/sewing: Cut with sharp shears in long strokes.

Care: Use a vacuum cleaner brush attachment to remove dust
from textured folds in shades and drapes to reduce the need
for washing. Wash before making up to prevent shrinking.

Organdy

Description: A fine, sheer, crisp cotton fabric in a plain weave.
It is lightweight yet strong and has a smooth surface.

Suitable use: Organdy is a lightweight, stiff fabric, making it
more suited to plain and simple window dressings rather
than functional curtains to keep out the light.

Cutting/sewing: Cut with long, clean sweeps of the scissors
to give a smooth edge and sew with a fine (size 9) machine
needle. Narrow seams, such as French seams, are a good
option as the fabric is sheer.

Care: Wash by hand or choose a gentle machine wash cycle,
and iron while damp as organdy creases badly.

Lace

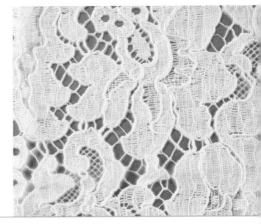

Description: Lace varies depending on its construction, but it is a sheer, open fabric with characteristic holes in a pattern or design. It is available as fabric or as edging lace in a range of widths so it can also be used as a trim.

Suitable use: Window dressings, table coverings, bedding, and soft drapes and shades.

Cutting/sewing: Make sure the right side of the fabric is recognized (it has a raised texture) and is used accordingly. Be aware of the pattern and match as you would a printed fabric. Sew with a fine standard needle and join with narrow seams.

Care: Hand-wash.

Voile

Description: A thin, lightweight transparent fabric constructed in a plain weave. It has a crisp handle and can be made from cotton or synthetic fibers. Voile is sometimes plain but usually has a printed pattern.

Suitable use: Voile is a good choice for sheer drapes at windows and over beds as it hangs well.

Cutting/sewing: Use long-bladed scissors for a smooth cut and sew with a new fine needle.

Care: Polyester voile washes and dries easily. Cotton voile should be ironed while damp to remove any creases.

Taffeta

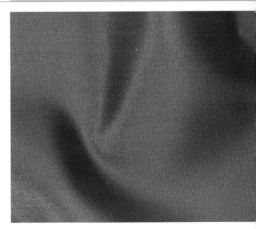

Description: A smooth, firm, woven fabric that can be made from a variety of fibers, including natural silk and synthetics or synthetic blends. It has a crisp texture and a characteristic sheen.

Suitable use: Curtains, pillows, and lampshades.

Cutting/sewing: Taffeta has a tendency to ravel, so using a wider seam allowance or neatening the raw edges with a serger may be helpful.

Care: For best results, dry-clean. Synthetic taffeta will wear better than 100 percent silk.

Dupion

Description: Dupion (or dupioni) is a woven cloth originally made from silk but now available in man-made fibers. The uneven thickness of the yarns creates a textured surface to the dull sheen of the fabric. Synthetic dupion often has a satin finish on the wrong side.

Suitable use: Curtains and shades as well as bedspreads and pillows.

Cutting/sewing: Cut with care as dupion can ravel badly, and sew with a new standard machine needle (size 9 to 11).

Care: Dry-clean, especially if drapes are lined.

Organza

Description: Made from silk, organza is a strong fabric as the yarns are highly spun; however, it is also lightweight and sheer.

Suitable use: Simple styled curtains and Austrian or festoon shades where the crispness of the fabric is needed to give a bunched appearance.

Cutting/sewing: Sew with a fine (size 9) standard needle and, as with organdy, choose narrow seams as the fabric is sheer.

Care: Wash by hand and iron while damp.

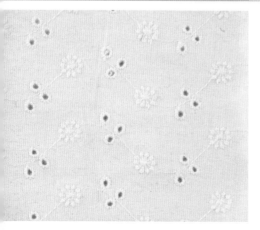

Broderie anglaise

Description: A form of lace with cutwork embroidery on a cotton or polyester/cotton fabric base. It is available as a fabric and also as an edge trimming, which is often gathered for a frilled effect.

Suitable use: Broderie anglaise is a soft fabric more suited to festoon or Austrian shades and gently draping curtains. Use it also for pillows and bedding.

Cutting/sewing: Cut with sharp shears.

Care: Use a vacuum cleaner brush attachment to remove dust from textured folds in shades and drapes to reduce the need for washing. Wash bedding and pillows in a washing machine as necessary.

Net and tulle

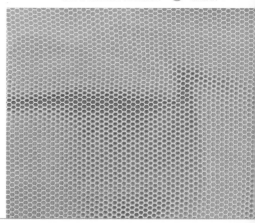

Description: Net is a mesh of threads forming a crisp, light, and open-weave fabric, while tulle is a finer mesh with a slightly softer handle.

Suitable use: Use net and tulle for window dressings to allow light into a room but still give some privacy. Simple tab top curtains and café-style threaded onto a pole work well.

Cutting/sewing: Cover the cutting surface with a cotton sheet to anchor the net or tulle and prevent it from slipping. Sew with a fine sewing machine needle (size 9 or 11) and choose narrow seams.

Care: Cool machine wash.

Thai silk

Description: A lightweight, plain weave fabric with an uneven surface created by slubs in the weft threads. It has a lustrous surface and is similar to silk dupion.

Suitable use: Pillows and drapes look good made from Thai silk. Use it for lampshades too.

Cutting/sewing: The appearance of Thai silk can vary depending on the direction from which the light catches it, so make sure the pieces are all cut in the same direction. Use a new fine needle when machining.

Care: Dry-clean or hand-wash for best results.

Muslin

Description: A strong, firm, plain weave cotton fabric that often is unbleached.

Suitable use: Muslin is often used as an underlayer for furnishings or for covering mattresses. It can also be used for drapes and shades.

Cutting/sewing: Easy to sew with. Cut with scissors and sew with a standard size 11 needle.

Care: Washing will cause shrinking and often alters the texture of the cloth. Iron while damp.

Mediumweight fabrics

Some mediumweight fabrics are strong (e.g. linen) while others are soft and delicate (e.g. cotton lawn) or even smooth (e.g. satin) or textured (e.g. brocade). They include plain-woven materials as well as decorative ones, with surface interest produced by the type of weave, applied finish, or printed design. Mediumweight fabrics are the most versatile and can be used for a huge range of projects.

GENERAL ADVICE

• Check the entire length of fabric for flaws, pulled threads, or light damage before starting to cut out.

• You may need to pre-wash or steam the fabric if the finished item is to be hand-washed when completed, otherwise it will need to be dry-cleaned.

• As 100 percent silk fabrics deteriorate in direct sunlight, it is important to line silk curtains or carefully consider their location.

• It may be necessary to snip or remove the selvage. If making curtains, this would be done after they are assembled.

• Plain and flat fell seams are good choices for mediumweight fabrics (see pages 54 and 56).

• Most mediumweight fabrics are best sewn with a size 11 needle.

• For most mediumweight fabrics, choose a straight stitch with a length of 2.5mm (10 stitches per inch).

• Neaten raw edges, which may ravel through wear or laundering.

• For fabrics with a special finish, make sure the method of cleaning is appropriate as washing can remove some finishes.

Plains

Examples: Sheeting, cotton lawn, linen, flannelette, polyester.

Use for: Bed linen, including sheets, duvets, bed skirts, curtains, pillows, shades, lampshades, tablecloths.

Avoid: Elaborate and decorative projects that require pattern and color unless they are used to coordinate with them. Also avoid light frothy styles, which are better suited to sheers and laces.

Textured weaves

Examples: Brocade, damask, raw silk (noil), seersucker, silk dupion.

Use for: Drapes, decorative pillows, lampshades, bedspreads/quilts, slipcovers, table linen.

Avoid: Austrian and festoon shades where the textured surface will collect dust and require more maintenance to keep the fabric clean.

Patterned or "finished" fabrics

Examples: Batik, brocade, chintz, gingham, moiré.

Use for: Drapes, shades, quilts, pillows, lampshades, slipcovers, and stronger qualities for upholstery.

Avoid: Minimalist styles.

Gingham

Description: Recognized by its checks, gingham is a woven fabric generally made from cotton or polyester/cotton. Some of the threads are dyed and the resulting plain weave fabric has squares or stripes of white and a color.

Suitable use: Café-style curtains, tablecloths, pillows, sheets, and duvet covers.

Cutting/sewing: Make sure the stripes and squares are matched appropriately and use a walking foot attachment to ensure the pattern matches when sewing seams.

Care: Gingham is easy to wash.

Sheeting

Description: Sheeting is available in cotton or cotton/polyester in a range of colors. It is produced on a wider than normal loom so that it can be used for bedding.

Suitable use: Sheets, bed skirts, duvets, and pillows.

Cutting/sewing: Sheeting is easy to handle and sew, especially if it is made of 100 percent cotton fibers.

Care: Machine washable. Cotton/polyester mixes wash and dry easily and need little ironing. Iron cotton sheeting while damp to remove any creases.

Damask

Description: Damask refers to the pattern created in the weave by a jacquard loom. It was traditionally made in linen, in a self-color, for tablecloths and napkins, although it is also available in cotton, silk, and polyester.

Suitable use: Tablecloths and napkins.

Cutting/sewing: Damask is easy to sew but be aware of the pattern when cutting out.

Care: Depending on the fiber content, damask may be machine-washed or require more delicate washing. The surface satin threads of the design can be damaged.

Cotton sateen

Description: Sateen is a woven cotton cloth with a satin weave. The long surface threads reflect light and, if mercerized, have great strength and luster.

Suitable use: The best curtain linings are made from cotton sateen and slightly heavier weights are often used to trim Roman shades, curtains, and valances, and it comes in an enormous range of colors.

Cutting/sewing: Care must be taken when cutting linings to ensure they are square, but the heavier weights are easy to handle and cut.

Care: Most types are washable, but allow for shrinkage.

Cambric

Description: A closely woven, plain weave fabric made from cotton. It is strong with a soft surface sheen, which adds a little stiffening.

Suitable use: A permanent inner cover for pillow forms and duvets.

Cutting/sewing: Cambric is easy to handle and manipulate. Cut with shears and sew with a standard size 11 needle.

Care: Wash and iron while damp to remove the creases.

Moiré

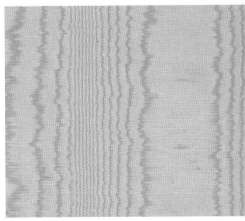

Description: Moiré refers to the watermark finish applied to the surface of a fabric whether it is cotton, silk, or synthetic in content.

Suitable use: Curtains, pillows, and lightweight upholstery.

Cutting/sewing: Handling will depend on the fiber content of the moiré-finished fabric.

Care: Washing will remove the moiré finish on the fabric's surface, so it will help if you vacuum to remove dust from furniture. Dry-clean curtains and pillow covers.

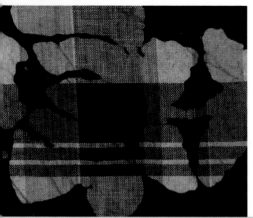

Batik

Description: Batik refers to the distinctive pattern created by resist dyeing normally on mediumweight woven cotton fabric.

Suitable use: Often used for patchwork and quilt projects, batik is suitable for bedding, pillows, tablecloths, and decorative hangings.

Cutting/sewing: Batik is simple to cut and sew as it is stable and easy to manipulate. The abstract design created by the dyeing process makes pattern matching unnecessary. Use a roller blade and self-healing mat when cutting patchwork pieces.

Care: Pre-shrink batik and be aware that the dyes may bleed when washing, so wash separately.

Flannelette

Description: Flannelette is a light- to mediumweight cotton fabric with a warm napped surface.

Suitable use: It is often used for bed sheets and pillowcases as its soft napped surface makes it warm and comfortable.

Cutting/sewing: When joining flannelette, make sure all the pieces have been cut and are lying in the same direction because of the napped surface.

Care: Easy to wash and keep clean.

Poplin

Description: Poplin, generally made from cotton, has a crossways ribbed texture on its surface. It is a strong and durable fabric that does not wrinkle.

Suitable use: Curtains, Roman shades, and pillows.

Cutting/sewing: Its cotton fiber content makes poplin easy to handle and sew with. Use a standard size 11 needle when machining.

Care: Poplin is easy to wash and iron.

Raw silk (noil)

Description: This is a cheaper silk fabric that uses the shorter waste fibers, and the resulting woven cloth is characteristically rough and uneven but has a dull sheen on its surface. It is available in a variety of weights but tends to ravel easily.

Suitable use: Raw silk is ideal for pillows and some upholstery projects. Use it for lampshades also.

Cutting/sewing: The raw edges need to be neatened to prevent raveling, but otherwise raw silk is easy to handle.

Care: Hand-wash colored silks separately as the colors may bleed, or dry-clean.

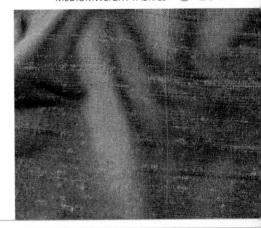

Sateen

Description: Sateen is a woven cotton cloth with a satin weave. The long surface threads reflect light as a dull sheen. It is available in plain colors and in a range of weights.

Suitable use: Lightweight sateen is used for lining curtains, while heavier weights are used for the curtains themselves.

Cutting/sewing: Sateen is an easy fabric to work with. Use sharp shears and cut with long sweeps to achieve a smooth cut edge. Use a standard needle to sew with.

Care: Sateen on its own may be washed, but if machined in as a lining it is advisable to have curtains dry-cleaned.

Viscose

Description: Viscose refers to the fiber content of the fabric rather than being a fabric in its own right. It is man-made derived from natural sources. It is generally blended with other fibers to gain a mixture of benefits as it is soft and drapes well but tends to crease.

Suitable use: Fabrics containing viscose can be used for curtains, pillows, and slipcovers.

Cutting/sewing: Viscose has a tendency to wrinkle, but any creases will iron out easily.

Care: Due to viscose's tendency to wrinkle, dry-cleaning is the best option.

Brocade

Description: A stiff, woven fabric with a surface pattern of threads created on a jacquard loom. Brocade can be self-colored or have several colored threads incorporated in the design. It can be made from cotton, silk, or synthetic fibers.

Suitable use: Traditional curtains as it drapes well. It is also good for pillows and upholstery, especially if it is made from synthetic fibers that are hardwearing.

Cutting/sewing: As brocade ravels badly, use wide seam allowances and neaten the raw edges appropriately. Use a standard size 11 or 14 needle.

Care: Some brocades may be washed, but this depends on the fiber content. If you are unsure, dry-clean brocade items.

Polyester

Description: Polyester refers to the fiber content of the fabric and is available in a range of weights, weaves, and finishes. It produces a hardwearing cloth, although it has a tendency to "pill" with abrasion, so it is often blended with other fibers.

Suitable use: Curtains, linings, shades, and pillows.

Cutting/sewing: Polyester is springy and can be difficult to handle.

Care: Polyester fabrics are easy to wash and they dry quickly.

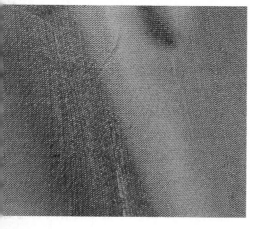

Silk dupion

Description: The uneven thickness of the natural silk threads creates a textured surface and a dull sheen to the fabric.

Suitable use: Curtains and shades, as well as for bedspreads and decorative pillows.

Cutting/sewing: Cut with care as silk dupion can ravel badly. Sew with a new (hence sharp) standard machine needle (size 9 to 11).

Care: Dry-clean, especially if drapes are lined.

Cretonne

Description: Plain or printed, cretonne looks similar to chintz without the surface glaze. It is also slightly heavier and better wearing.

Suitable use: Most home décor projects, as it is washable and fairly hardwearing.

Cutting/sewing: Pre-shrink before cutting out. Cretonne is easy to handle and sew. Use a standard needle in a size 14. A walking foot attachment to the sewing machine will help with pattern matching.

Care: Wash by hand or machine as necessary.

Microfiber

Description: This fine, synthetic fiber filament is available in a range of weights and finishes (e.g. suede, sand). It does not "pill" and can take special treatments, making it possible for fabrics to repel dirt and water. It drapes well and doesn't crease.

Suitable use: Tablecloths, upholstery, pillows, and curtains.

Cutting/sewing: Use sharp, long-bladed scissors and assume the fabric has a nap. Sew with a fine, microtex needle that is specially designed for microfiber fabrics, and use polyester thread.

Care: Machine wash but do not use fabric conditioner as this may leave marks.

Chintz

Description: Chintz is a closely woven cotton fabric with a glaze or sheen on the surface as a result of an applied resin or mechanical finish. It is either plain or printed, often with large floral designs.

Suitable use: Upholstery, curtains, decorative pillows, and tablecloths.

Cutting/sewing: Chintz is easy to cut, sew, and handle. Pattern matching on long curtain seams can be helped by using a walking foot attachment on the sewing machine.

Care: Dry-clean and press on the wrong side with a warm iron.

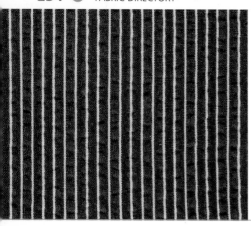

Seersucker

Description: This decorative cloth has a distinctive bubble texture with flat and crinkled stripes or squares. Traditionally made from cotton, it is now often mixed with polyester.

Suitable use: Use seersucker for tablecloths and napkins, and less formal curtain styles.

Cutting/sewing: Use larger seam allowances as the edge may not be quite straight when cutting into the crinkled fabric. Take care when using the iron between sewing processes as this will flatten the fabric's three-dimensional texture.

Care: Washes easily, but hover a steam iron over the fabric if necessary without applying pressure.

Cotton lawn

Description: A fine, smooth, plain weave fabric with a soft, crisp finish. It can be plain or printed.

Suitable use: The fine, lightweight nature makes cotton lawn suitable for soft shades, light curtains, bedding, tablecloths, and napkins.

Cutting/sewing: Choose a standard size 11 needle for machine sewing. For a decorative, heirloom finish to edge tablecloths and napkins, sew with a wing needle and a blanket stitch.

Care: Cotton lawn washes easily. Iron while damp to remove any creases.

Satin

Description: Satin, whether made from cotton, silk, or synthetic fibers, has a beautifully shiny appearance due to the long threads that lie on the surface and reflect light. The surface threads can be damaged easily, but cotton satin is more durable than silk.

Suitable use: Bedspreads, pillows, and sumptuous curtains and shades.

Cutting/sewing: Cutting satin can be difficult as it is slippery to handle, so place it on a cotton sheet rather than on a shiny tabletop. Sew with a new fine needle to avoid damaging the fabric threads.

Care: Satin can become stained or damaged easily, so choose its location and use carefully.

Linen

Description: Linen is an ancient fabric made from the stems of the flax plant that are processed to create a strong, crisp cloth. It is generally woven in a plain, twill, or damask weave.

Suitable use: Traditional tablecloths, and napkins, pillows, and slipcovers.

Cutting/sewing: Easy to handle and sew.

Care: Linen wrinkles badly unless it is pre-treated. Wash or dry-clean.

Ticking

Description: This is a strong cotton, twill fabric that is closely woven and traditionally recognized with black-and-white stripes.

Suitable use: Mattress and pillow covers. Ticking can also be used as an upholstery fabric on simple shaped designs such as deckchairs and directors' chairs.

Cutting/sewing: As ticking is densely woven, it is very coarse and difficult to sew.

Care: If possible, vacuum or wipe the surface of ticking rather than removing it to wash.

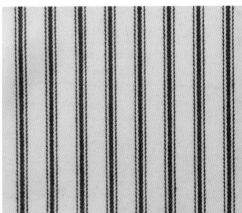

Printed cotton

Description: One hundred percent cotton or mixed with synthetic fibers to add crease resistance and drape to the properties of the natural fiber. Can be light- through to heavyweight.

Suitable use: One of the most popular and versatile fabrics for shades, pillows, and curtains—from floaty unlined to lined and interlined.

Cutting/sewing: Follow the pattern repeat, use an 80–90 machine needle, depending on weight of fabric.

Care: One hundred percent cotton may need to be prewashed before cutting, or allow for shrinkage. (Prewashing may remove the "finish" from new fabrics; steam pressing can be an alternative.)

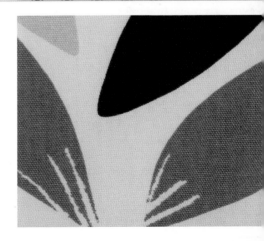

Heavyweight fabrics

These strong, thick fabrics can be difficult to handle and sew. Some are soft and others stiff, some have interesting textures (e.g. tapestry) and others smooth surfaces (e.g. vinyl, leather). Some heavyweight fabrics have a pile (e.g. velvet, corduroy) making them bulky to handle and giving a "direction" so that it is necessary to cut and hang the pieces the same way. They are well suited to upholstery projects and functional curtains that insulate well and keep out the light.

GENERAL ADVICE

- Cut pile and napped fabrics so that all pieces lie in the same direction.
- Cut animal skins using the position of the spine as the grain.
- Keep the vacuum cleaner close by when cutting a pile fabric as the loose fibers can be a problem.
- As heavyweight fabrics made from 100 percent silk deteriorate in direct sunlight, it is important to add a lining to silk curtains or carefully consider their location.
- It may be necessary to cut off the selvage before sewing the curtain panels together, and use a French seam (see page 55) to enclose all the raw edges.
- Choose flat seams that will not add unnecessary bulk to thick and heavy fabrics.
- Sew with an appropriate and strong needle—e.g. size 14/16/18, a jeans needle, or leather needle (for leather and suede).
- Increase the stitch length to approximately 8 stitches per inch (3mm) to cope with the density of the fabric.
- Reduce the pressure of the presser foot or attach a walking foot to the sewing machine. This will prevent the layers of fabric shifting when sewing seams.
- Clean upholstery fabrics in place with a vacuum cleaner and appropriate cleaner. If the fabrics can be removed, dry-clean them and only wash if the instructions indicate suitability.

Animal skins

Examples: Leather, suede.
Use for: Upholstery, beanbags, headboards.
Avoid: Soft draping curtain styles, pillows, festoon shades, bed linen.

Stiff

Examples: Buckram, blackout lining, burlap.
Use for: Supporting other fabrics.
Avoid: Delicate and draped styles.

Fabrics with a pile

Examples: Corduroy, velvet, velveteen.
Use for: Upholstery, slipcovers, warm and heavy formal curtains, headboards, beanbags, throws.
Avoid: Delicate curtains/ drapes, Austrian shades, bed linen, tablecloths.

Strong

Examples: Denim, corduroy, canvas, leather, upholstery fabric.
Use for: Upholstery, slipcovers, drapes, Roman shades, covering headboards.
Avoid: Soft draping curtains, sheets, duvet covers, pillows.

Felt

Description: Felt is a bonded fabric produced direct from fibers matted together rather than being woven or knitted. It is not a strong fabric.

Suitable use: Although it is not a strong fabric, felt can be used as a protective layer over tables, or its bright colors can be used for appliqué decoration on home decoration projects.

Cutting/sewing: Felt has no right side or grain, making it easy and economical to cut with little waste.

Care: Washing will cause it to disintegrate, so dry-clean if necessary.

Tartan

Description: Tartan is a traditional, Scottish woolen twill weave cloth with a distinctive plaid or check design. The fabric threads are dyed, then woven to create specific designs.

Suitable use: Tartan is popular for curtains, but it can also be used for slipcovers and pillows.

Cutting/sewing: Pattern matching is essential and a walking foot helps to achieve this.

Care: Dry-clean for best results.

Buckram

Description: This is a loosely woven cloth but stiffened with glue.

Suitable use: Buckram is used as an interlining (underlining) to back fabrics for pelmets and tiebacks, to give them more body.

Cutting/sewing: Cut pieces minus the seam allowances and use weights rather than pins to secure the cloth when cutting.

Care: Buckram cannot be washed.

Mohair

Description: From the Angora goat, this fiber produces a beautifully soft, warm, and silky fabric. It is durable and resilient but very expensive, so it is often mixed with other fibers.

Suitable use: Mohair makes wonderful decorative pillows that are warm and soft.

Cutting/sewing: Arrange all cut pieces in the same direction and sew with polyester thread.

Care: Hand-wash.

Corduroy

Description: Cord is a woven fabric recognized by the ridges or wales that run the length of the cloth. It is normally made from cotton and comes in a range of weights from fine needlecord for dressmaking to heavier fabric with broader wales for upholstery. It is strong and hardwearing.

Suitable use: Some weights are suitable for upholstery but heavy wear will flatten the pile. Use corduroy for curtains and pillows too.

Cutting/sewing: Make sure all panels hang in the same direction as the color appears different, depending on how the light hits the pile. Neaten the raw edges as it tends to ravel. A walking foot may make sewing easier.

Care: Take care when ironing corduroy as the pile may become flattened.

Denim

Description: This traditional workwear fabric is a strong cotton cloth in a twill weave. Usually, it has blue warp threads and white weft threads, giving its characteristic appearance. It is a stiff, hardwearing fabric, but it can be softened to make it more versatile. It is available in various weights.

Suitable use: Slipcovers, upholstery, curtains, and pillows.

Cutting/sewing: Lighter, softer denims are easy to cut and sew, but heavier weights will prove more difficult. Sew with a "jeans" needle, which is designed for use on denim.

Care: Denim is machine washable but washing will reduce the intensity of the color and produce a softer handle.

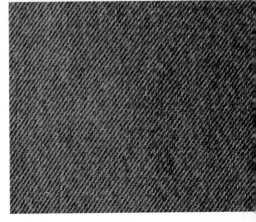

Burlap

Description: A harsh and loosely woven cloth made from hemp or jute, and traditionally used for sacking.

Suitable use: Use it for pillows, curtains, and shades for its texture and rustic quality.

Cutting/sewing: Working with burlap can be harsh on the hands, and it can be difficult to manipulate and sew. Burlap ravels badly.

Care: Burlap will shrink on washing, so it's a good idea to prewash it. Ironing can cause distortion of the weave. Dry-cleaning is recommended.

Tapestry

Description: Tapestry is a hardwearing and decorative fabric, elaborately patterned.

Suitable use: As tapestry fabric is durable, use it for upholstery on sofas and chairs. It is also suitable for pillows and drapes.

Cutting/sewing: Cut with sharp shears and match the pattern at the seams. Sew with a strong needle and use a walking foot to help cope with layers of this thick fabric.

Care: Vacuum with a brush attachment in position and dry-clean when necessary. Tapestry fabric is often treated to prevent staining.

Jacquard tapestry

Description: This elaborately patterned and colored cloth is made on a jacquard loom. It is heavyweight, making it a strong, decorative fabric.

Suitable use: Upholstery, pillows, and rich-looking curtains.

Cutting/sewing: Cut with sharp shears and match the pattern at the seams. Sew with a strong needle and use a walking foot to help cope with the thick fabric.

Care: Vacuum with a brush attachment in position and dry-clean when necessary.

Leather

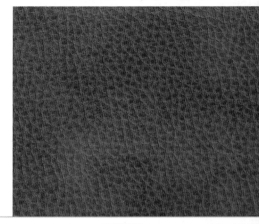

Description: Leather is animal skin treated and sometimes dyed. It varies in texture and thickness and comes in small pieces. Synthetic leather imitation fabrics are also available.

Suitable use: Leather is popular for upholstering sofas and covering headboards.

Cutting/sewing: Mark the shapes required on the wrong side of the leather and cut with a craft knife with a protective board below. Sew with a leather needle, which is specially sharpened to cut through the animal skin, and with strong polyester or buttonhole thread. Increase the stitch length and glue rather than sew where necessary.

Care: Clean with a leather cleaner.

Plastic/vinyl

Description: Vinyl is often applied as a layer to a backing of cotton, which gives it additional strength, but it can be used as a fabric itself. The color and texture can be made to give the appearance of leather, or it can be plain or even clear. It is waterproof and practical.

Suitable use: Plastic or vinyl is ideal for seat covers in the kitchen or garden, and it is very popular for tablecloths. Lightweight plastic can be used for shower curtains.

Cutting/sewing: Use weights or sticky tape rather than pins. Vinyl, without a backing, lacks strength and needle holes can perforate and weaken it, so choose its use wisely.

Care: Plastic wipes clean.

Tweed

Description: Traditionally, tweed was a wool cloth woven in two or more colors. It is now often made from a blend of fibers and is warm with a coarse texture.

Suitable use: Use tweed for curtains/drapes as it hangs well and for its insulation qualities. Suitable for casual throws and pillows, too.

Cutting/sewing: If the tweed has a pattern, cut and join panels carefully.

Care: Hand-wash or dry-clean. Use a vacuum cleaner regularly to remove dust from large curtains.

Blackout lining

Description: Blackout fabric is not actually black but comes in neutral colors. It is used to exclude light, reduce noise, and improve insulation.

Suitable use: Ideal for Roman shades as it adds weight and depth to the chosen fabric. It does not drape well and therefore is not suitable for all curtains—it works well for large, heavy drapes but will be too stiff for smaller windows.

Cutting/sewing: A larger machine needle (size 14/16) will be required to sew blackout fabric. Some types have a surface that may stick to the machine when sewing, so try sprinkling talcum powder over it to allow it to run through smoothly.

Care: Wipe the surface or hand-wash curtains with blackout lining if appropriate.

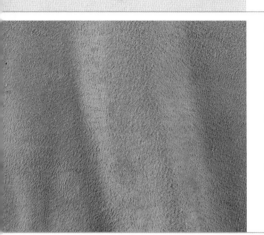

Suede

Description: Suede is the inside of an animal skin (e.g. cowhide, pigskin, or lambskin). Synthetic suede is now popular as it is realistic, easier to launder, and comes on the roll (not small pieces).

Suitable use: Suede and faux suede are ideal fabrics for curtains, lampshades, upholstery, and slipcovers.

Cutting/sewing: Cut real suede using the backbone position as the straight grain. Cut with a craft knife or scissors if soft enough. Sew with a leather needle. Faux suede can be cut and sewn easily.

Care: Treat suede with a leather-cleaner. Faux suede can often be machine washed, but check the laundry instructions first.

Rep

Description: Rep is a hardwearing fabric with a distinctive rib across it. It is often made from cotton or a cotton mix.

Suitable use: Its strength makes rep ideal for upholstery and slipcovers.

Cutting/sewing: Rep tends to ravel badly, so try neatening the raw edges before sewing panels together. Make sure the distinctive rib is used consistently in the same direction.

Care: Dry-cleaning is recommended.

Worsted

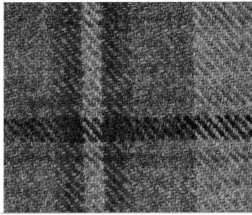

Description: A worsted yarn has long wool fibers combed and highly twisted to give a smooth, strong finish. It is woven in a plain or twill weave. It is hardwearing and resilient.

Suitable use: Worsted wool is ideal for upholstery and slipcovers because of its strength.

Cutting/sewing: Sew with polyester thread and a standard needle. Protect the surface of the fabric with a pressing cloth.

Care: It is better if worsted wool is pre-shrunk and stain treated before being used for upholstery. Dry-clean.

Canvas

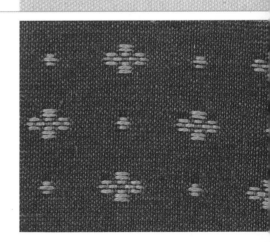

Description: Canvas is a very strong and coarse cotton fabric sometimes referred to as duck cloth.

Suitable use: Its strength and rigidity make canvas suitable only for upholstering deckchairs and directors' chairs, but some lighter weights can be sewn and used for simple curtains.

Cutting/sewing: It is too heavy and stiff to sew on a domestic machine. Try lighter weights with a strong size 16 needle.

Care: If the canvas can be removed from its fixings, wash on a gentle cycle in the washing machine and return while still damp. If it cannot be removed, use a spray upholstery cleaner.

Upholstery fabric

Description: There are many varieties of upholstery fabric, but it is always strong, tough, and hardwearing.

Suitable use: In addition to upholstery uses, it can also be made into slipcovers, pillows, drapes, and shades.

Cutting/sewing: Upholstery fabric is difficult to cut and sew as it is quite tough. Cut in a single layer and sew with a size 14/16 needle. Increase the stitch length to accommodate the dense fabric and use a walking foot attachment.

Care: Vacuum to reduce the dust and dry-clean.

Velvet

Description: Velvet is a woven fabric with a dense pile on the right side. It can be made from cotton, silk, man-made, or synthetic fibers, and is available in a range of weights.

Suitable use: Most popular for curtains, velvet can also be used for pillows and casual throws.

Cutting/sewing: Mark the fabric pieces on the wrong side with chalk and cut from the wrong side. Make sure all panels lie in the same direction. Fit a walking foot to the sewing machine to avoid "fabric creep" and choose a size 14/16 needle and a longer straight stitch. Cotton velvet is much easier to handle than polyester velvet. Iron carefully from the wrong side over a spare piece of velvet or a velvet board.

Care: Vacuum and dry-clean.

Velveteen

Description: With a similar appearance to velvet, velveteen has a shorter brushed pile and is more durable.

Suitable use: Choose velveteen for slipcovers, pillows, beanbags, and curtains/drapes. It is more durable than velvet and can take more wear.

Cutting/sewing: Velveteen is easy to handle and sew, but all panels must be cut to lie in the same direction because of its napped surface.

Care: Dry-clean.

Drill

Description: Drill is a strong and hardwearing cotton or cotton/polyester fabric with a diagonal, twill weave.

Suitable use: Simple curtains and Roman shades, and slipcovers, beanbags, and pillows.

Cutting/sewing: Use sharp shears in long sweeping strokes to produce a smooth edge. Sew with a strong size 14 or 16 needle.

Care: Wash by machine or by hand.

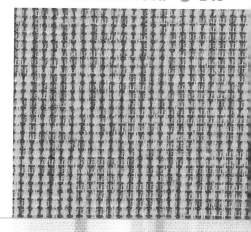

Chenille

Description: The yarn has a velvety texture, so the resulting cloth has a soft tufted pile. It is a thick and warm fabric and can be made from wool, cotton, or synthetic fibers.

Suitable use: The soft, springy varieties can be used for throws and pillows, but the heavier weights are used for curtains or upholstery.

Cutting/sewing: Easy to handle and cut out. Sew using 80–100-size needles depending on the weight.

Care: Treat as velvet (pile) when pressing. Most cases would require dry-cleaning.

Linen union

Description: A blend of linen and mixed fibers, usually cotton. Linen union has the look of linen but is less prone to creasing. It is hardwearing.

Suitable use: Linen union is ideal for full-length curtains, pillows, and seat covers.

Cutting/sewing: Usually printed designs, so the pattern repeat must be followed across the width. Sew with a 90 machine needle.

Care: Dry-clean.

Resources

Associations

American Sewing Guild
www.asg.org
Suite 510, 9660 Hillcroft
Houston, TX 77096
Tel: 713-729-3000
A nonprofit organization for people who sew

Sewing.org
www.sewing.org
Sewing & Craft Alliance
P.O. Box 369
Monroeville, PA 15146
Tel: 412-372-5950
A nonprofit organization with the aim to get people sewing

Window Coverings
Association of America
www.wcaa.org
WCAA Main Office
2646 Hwy 109, Suite 205
Grover, MO 63040
Tel: 636-273-4090; Toll-free: 888-298-9222
A nonprofit organization with a dealer directory

Materials
Fabrics

Benartex Inc.
www.benartex.com
1359 Broadway, Suite 110
New York, NY 10018
Tel: 212-921-8204
Email: info@benartex.com
Original cotton fabrics

Blendworth
www.blendworth.co.uk
Crookley Park, Horndean
Hampshire PO8 0AD, U.K.
Tel: +44-(0)23-9259-4911
Email: mail@blendworth.co.uk
Luxury fabrics

Colefax and Fowler
www.colefax.com
Head Office, 19-23 Grosvenor Hill
London W1K 3QD, U.K.
Tel: +44-(0)20-7318-6000
Sophisticated English style

Harlequin Harris
www.harlequin.uk.com
Harlequin Harris Showroom
Chelsea Harbour Design Centre
Chelsea, London SW10 0XE, U.K.
Tel: +44-(0)8708-300032
Email: enquiries@harlequinharris.com
Luxury fabrics

J.R. Burrows & Company
www.burrows.com
P.O. Box 522, Rockland
Massachusetts 02370
Tel: 800-347-1795
Email: merchant@burrows.com
Traditional English prints and lace

Laura Ashley
www.lauraashley.com
PO Box 19, Newtown
Powys SY16 1DZ, U.K.
Tel: +44-(0)871-230-2301
Variety of quality fabrics

Linwood
www.linwoodfabric.com
15 Headlands Business Park
Salisbury Road, Ringwood
Hampshire BH24 3PB, U.K.
Tel: +44-(0)1425-461176
Email: sales@linwoodfabric.com
Elegant and classic fabrics

Malabar
www.malabar.co.uk
31-33, The South Bank Business Centre
Ponton Road, London SW8 5BL, U.K.
Tel: +44-(0)20-7501-4200
Email: info@malabar.co.uk
Bright, India-inspired fabrics

Morton, Young & Borland
www.myb-ltd.com
Newmilns, Ayrshire KA16 9AL
Scotland, U.K.
Tel: +44-(0)1560-321210
Email: info@myb-ltd.com
Fine lace and madras

Romo Fabrics/Villa Nova
www.romofabrics.com
Head Office
Lowmoor Rd, Kirky-in-Ashfield
Nottinghamshire NG17 7DE, U.K.
Tel: +44-(0)1623-756699
Exclusive fabric collections

Sanderson
www.sandersonfabrics.co.uk
Sanderson Interiors
118-130 Kings Road, Harrogate
North Yorkshire HG1 5HY, U.K.
Tel: +44-(0)1423-500051
Email: sales@sandersonfabrics.co.uk
Quality fabrics

Stark Fabric
www.starkfabric.com
D&D Building, 979 Third Avenue
10th Floor, New York, NY 10022-1276
Tel: 212-355-7186
Designer fabric collection

Fabrics and hardware

Smith & Noble
www.smithandnoble.com
Tel: 800-248-8888
Email: contactus@smithnoble.com

Fabrics and trimmings

Osborne & Little Inc.
www.osborneandlittle.com
90 Commerce Rd
Stamford, CT 06902
Tel: 203-359-1500

Waverly
www.waverly.com

Fabrics, hardware, and trimmings

Calico Corners
www.calicocorners.com
Customer Service, 203 Gale Lane
Kennett Square, PA 19348
Tel: 1-800-213-6366

Country Curtains
www.countrycurtains.com
Red Lion Inn, P.O. Box 955
Stockbridge, Massachusetts 01262
Tel: 1-800-937-1237
Email: dearjane@countrycurtains.com

John Lewis
www.johnlewis.com
Customer Services, John Lewis Direct
P.O. Box 19615, Erskine PA8 6WU, U.K.
Tel: +44-(0)8456-049049

Price & Company (Regency) Ltd.
www.price-regency.co.uk
Regency House, North Street
Portslade, Brighton BN41 1ES, U.K.
Email: enquiries@price-regency.co.uk

Rufflette
www.rufflette.com
Rufflette Ltd, Sharston Rd
Manchester M22 4TH, U.K.
Tel: +44-(0)161-998-1811
Email: customer-care@rufflette.com

Stroheim & Romann, Inc.
www.stroheim.com
30-30 47th Avenue
New York, NY 11101
Tel: 718-706-7000
Email: info@stroheim.com

Hardware

The Bradley Collection, Inc.
www.bradleycollection.co.uk
3455 S. La Clenega Boulevard Suite A
Los Angeles, CA 90016
Tel: 310-815-8255
Email: info@bradleycollection.com
Distinctive high-quality drapery systems

Graber Blinds
www.graberblinds.com
Customer Service Center
Springs Window Fashions
8467 Route 405 Highway South
P.O. Box 500
Montgomery, PA 17752
Tel: 1-877-792-0002
Email: windowfashions@
springswindowfashions.com

Integra Products Ltd.
www.integra-products.co.uk
High Point, Sandy Hill Business Park
Sandy Way, Amington
Tamworth B77 4DU, U.K.
Tel: +44-(0)1543-267100
Email: cus.care@integra-products.co.uk

Kirsch Window Fashions
www.kirsch.com
Tel: Toll-free 1-800-817-6344

Hardware and trimmings

Croscill Home
www.croscill.com

Hunter & Hyland
www.hunterandhyland.co.uk
201–5 Kingston Rd, Leatherhead
Surrey KT22 7PB, U.K.
Tel: +44-(0)1372-378511

Trimmings

The Handsome Trimming Company Ltd.
www.handsometrimmings.co.uk
3A Skelmanthorpe Technology Park
Station Road
Skelmanthorpe HD8 9GA, U.K.
Tel: +44-(0)1484-862985
Email: info@handsometrimmings.co.uk

Home-Sew Inc.
P.O. Box 4099
Bethlehem, PA 18018
Tel: Toll-free 1-800-344-4739
Email: customerservice@homesew.com

Websites

Inspiration

Architectural Digest
www.architecturaldigest.com
Celebrity homes and exotic interiors

Better Homes and Gardens
www.bhg.com
Practical ideas for your home

Elle Décor
www.elledecor.com
Ideas for a trendy lifestyle with contemporary French influence

House Beautiful
www.housebeautiful.com
Practical ideas for your home

Romantic Homes
www.romantichomes.com
Add your personal touch of casual elegance

Style Will Save Us
www.stylewillsaveus.com
Quirky eco-friendly interiors ideas

Traditional Home
www.traditionalhome.com
Classic interiors and vintage ideas

Online magazines

isew
www.isew.co.uk
For sewing enthusiasts

Sew News
www.sewnews.com
Creative sewing for you and your home

Sewing World
www.sewingworldmagazine.com
All aspects of sewing

Threads
www.threadsmagazine.com
For sewing enthusiasts

Sewing machine companies

www.brother.com
www.elna.com
www.husqvarnaviking.com
www.janome.com
www.berinausa.com
www.babylock.com
www.pfaff.com
www.singer.com

Glossary

Austrian shade
Ruched shade that reefs up into scallops, operated by a cord system.

Basting
Long running hand or machine stitch used for temporarily holding layers of fabric together.

Batten
Thin piece of wood that slots into the base hem of a roller or Roman shade to ensure that the fabric hangs straight.

Batting
Thick cotton or polyester padding used in pillows, tiebacks, and quilting.

Bay window
Multiple window unit that forms an angled recess.

Bed skirt
A skirt that conceals the bed base and space underneath.

Blackout lining
Lining fabric that has been laminated to block out light.

Bolster
Cylindrical pillow.

Bow window
Multiple window unit that forms a curved recess.

Box cushion
Cushion made from two layers of fabric with a gusset between them.

Box pleat
Evenly spaced flat-fronted pleat, with two folds turned inward and sewn in place.

Curtain
Panel of fabric used to cover a window, suspended from rings, hooks, or tabs or with a gathered heading. See also *Drapery*.

Dormer window
Vertical window that projects from the sloping plane of a roof, often in an attic, forming an alcove in the interior.

Drapery
Formal window treatment consisting of a heavy panel of fabric, often lined and full length, with a pleated heading.

Eyelet
Metal ring lining a hole in fabric so that a rod can pass through. Used for headings and also as a decorative feature on blinds.

Flange
Flat, double-thickness fabric trim extending beyond the edges of a cushion.

French pleat
Three-fold pleat, also known as a pinch pleat.

Frill
Strip of gathered fabric.

Fringe, fringing
Decorative edging made of hanging threads or tassels.

Gathered heading
Informal heading in which fabric is drawn into soft folds by cords that run through a gathering tape sewn onto the reverse.

Goblet pleat
Heading in which the pleat is padded to form a rounded, puffed shape.

Heading
Any means by which fabric is gathered or pleated across the top and attached to a rod, track, or pole.

Holdbacks
Hardware mounted on the wall or window frame that functions like tiebacks to hold curtains back.

Interlining
Soft opaque fabric sewn between the main drapery fabric and the lining to block light, improve hang, and enhance insulation.

Miter
Finishing a corner with a diagonal fold.

Pelmet
Stiffened fabric that covers the top of a window, the track, and the heading of the curtain or shade.

Pilling
Through wear, small balls of fiber can appear on the surface of some fabrics. They can be picked or cut off.

Pin tucks
Very narrow tucks.

Pinch pleat
See *French pleat*.

Piping
Edge trim made of fabric and sewn into a seam.

Repeat
The distance between one motif and another in a pattern.

Rod pocket
Heading in which the fabric is turned over and sewn to form an open-ended channel into which a rod is inserted. Also known as a cased heading.

Roller shade
Flat shade made of fabric or vinyl, operated by a spring-mounted roller.

Roman shade
Fabric shade that raises into horizontal folds and is operated by cords sewn on the reverse of the fabric.

Seam allowance
Distance between the stitching line and the edge of the fabric when sewing pieces together.

Selvage
Finished edges of a cloth that do not ravel.

Shade
Any treatment made of fabric (or sometimes vinyl) that lifts and lowers against the windowpane.

Squab
Cushion cut to the shape of a chair seat.

Stackback
Space occupied by a curtain or drapery when it is fully open.

Tented tieback
Draperies tied back from the window in such a way as to reveal their lining.

Tieback
Shaped or stiffened fabric or ties used to hold curtains and draperies back from the window.

Trim, trimming
Decorative braid, fringe, or tassel that is used to embellish window treatments.

Valance
Top window treatment made of fabric, used on its own or to hide hardware.

Index

Credits

Quarto would like to thank the following agencies and manufacturers for kindly supplying images for inclusion in this book:

Blendworth
www.blendworth.co.uk
p1, 5

Colefax and Fowler
www.colefax.com
Courtesy of Jane Churchill Fabrics and Wallpapers (© Jane Churchill Fabrics and Wallpapers)
p120, 104, 106, 145, 178, 217

Osborne & Little
Stockist tel: (UK) 020 7352 1456
www.osborneandlittle.com
p4, 176, 174, 218

Harlequin
www.harlequin.uk.com
Stockist tel: (UK) 0844 543 0299
p2, 27, 29, 60

The Poles Company
www.thepolescompany.co.uk

Philips
www.philips.com

www.brother.co.uk/sewing

Rufflette
www.rufflette.com

Alamy
p10

www.shutterstock.com

All other images are the copyright of Quarto Publishing plc. While every effort has been made to credit contributors, Quarto would like to apologize should there have been any omissions or errors, and would be pleased to make the appropriate correction for future editions of the book.

Quarto would also like to thank the following companies for kindly supplying fabrics:

Laura Ashley, who provided fabrics for projects on pages 128, 131, 137, 138, 166, 171, 173, 187, 189, 191, 192
www.lauraashley.com

Alexander Furnishings who provided swatches for the Fabric directory
Tel: +44-(0)20-7935-8664
51–61 Wigmore Street, Marylebone, London W1U 1PU